dhyana ziegler and molefi kete asante

THUNDER AND SILENCE
the mass media in africa

Africa World Press, Inc.
P.O. Box 1892
Trenton, New Jersey 08607

Africa World Press, Inc.
P.O. Box 1892
Trenton, New Jersey 08607

Copyright © 1992 by Dhyana Ziegler and Molefi Kete Asante
First Printing 1992

All rights reserved. No part of this publication may be reproduced, stored in a retrieval system or transmitted in any form or by any means electronic, mechanical or otherwise without the prior written permission of the publisher.

Book design and typesetting by Malcolm Litchfield
This book is composed in Janson and Peignot

Cover Illustration by Carles J. Juzang

ISBN: 0-86543-250-3   Cloth
       0-86543-251-1   Paper

CONTENTS

		Preface	v
ONE		The Foundations	3
TWO		Newspapers and the Colonial Context	11
THREE		Media Control and National Development	29
FOUR		Electronic Broadcasting in Africa	55
FIVE		Two National Perspectives on the Media	74
SIX		Problems and Prerogatives	91
SEVEN		The Potential for Press Freedom	102
EIGHT		Access to International Information	114
NINE		The Media and Ideology: A Final Note	126
APPENDICES	A	The Leading Media Institutions in Africa	131
	B	Rural Newspapers in Africa	158
	C	African Media Facts by Region	160
	D	Electronic Broadcasting by Region	183
		References	195
		Index	201

preface

IN THE last few decades, there has been a tremendous growth of African media. This has meant new orientations to society, business, as well as domestic and international relationships. As nation after nation has thrown off the elements of their colonial or settler past in order to firmly locate their media institutions within the framework of African cultural systems, there have been some growing pains. And while we cannot speak of African media as perfectly mature at this point in history, we can certainly see that it has come a long way.

The aim of our book is to provide the general reader and the expert reader with a critical appraisal of the history, problems, and prospects for African media. It is not our intention to present a litany of the difficulties faced by the African media, although we are well aware of the fact that we could not write this book without reference to the remaining obstacles in most African societies. For a number of reasons elaborated in this book, we began to pay close attention to the nature of African media while training in communication. Both of us came to this work with backgrounds in communication and broadcasting theory, however, we recognized quite early that very little of our training prepared us to understand media in Africa. Consequently, we undertook to examine much of the literature about African

PREFACE

media and to conduct our own interviews and observations to re-tool ourselves as students of African media.

We have called the book *Thunder and Silence* inasmuch as we have seen in our review of the African media, moments of tremendous freedom, such as various periods in the Nigerian media when newspapers proliferated and media executives and writers were considered leaders in their own right, and periods of silence, such as in Ethiopia, where the press speaks ever so timidly. During the next few years, African media must become more sophisticated in order to deliver essential services to the people of the continent. A knowledge of the background of the media systems should assist Africans and others in predicting the next steps for a more developed media.

We hope this modest contribution will serve as an impetus for others to continue the conceptual development as well as the theoretical development of African media.

* * * * *

We would like to acknowledge Kathy Moore, Cora Smith, Marva Rudolph and Camille Hazeur for all their assistance in the preparation of this manuscript. We would not have been able to complete this work without their dedicated service. We also would like to thank our families for all of their love, support, inspiration, and understanding of the time that is needed to complete a task such as this one.

We dedicate this book to the African Diaspora.

Dhyana Ziegler
Molefi Kete Asante

thunder and silence

ONE

THE FOUNDATIONS

discovering a perspective

THE FOUNDATION of the modern systems of communications in the continent of Africa should be the traditional village communication systems. Indeed, no understanding of the contemporary philosophies of mass communication in Africa can be had without a full appreciation of the role of traditional aspects of communication. Thus, it is not entirely true as Dennis Wilcox has written that the nature of "press-government relationships in Africa . . . is . . . due to the legacy left by colonial administrators and governments." What Wilcox suggests along with others, particularly Malinowski (1966) is that the European influence on African communication media is the single most important aspect of the contemporary situation in the media on the continent. Certainly, the colonial legacy is significant, and in many areas responsible for the underdevelopment of Africa (Rodney 1974) but it would be a mistake to assume that media philosophies of most of Africa are founded only upon the colonial experience. If anything, it seems that many nations in Africa are seeking to repudiate their colonial legacies and searching for connections to the past. In one of the most telling decisions of an African

ONE

government, Nathan Shamuyarira, Minister of Information, Posts and Telecommunications for Zimbabwe, announced that employees of his ministry's post facilities would receive salary commensurate with ability to perform certain skills, not on the basis of certificates as had been the case under the Ian Smith government.

This line of reasoning is quite in keeping with the cultural policies and histories of most African nations. Inasmuch as European practices often contradicted the values of the indigenous people, new post-independence policies have been developed to augment the existing institutions and protocols of communication. K. M. Aithnard (1976, 9) expressed the concern of African nations most explicitly when he wrote of Togo's Cultural policy:

> Modernization is generally taken to mean the whole process by which a society enters the small circle of industrialized countries. For Africa, this process of change would be only a simple transposition of experience from the industrialized world to the African world and would be essentially exogenous in character. Togo, on the other hand, conceives of development as the establishment of internal conditions favoring endogenous production. Such development would be geared to the basic characteristics and values marking the human environment.

What Aithnard and other culturists are suggesting is that African development and modernization must be examined from an Afrocentric perspective. To understand how modern media systems developed, apart from the technical imitation of the industrialized nations, it is necessary to grasp the uses made of modern media by Africans, uses which are rooted in the historical and cultural foundations of each society.

The enviro-technical complexes of Abidjan, Nairobi, Lagos or Douala often conceal true myths, legends, and traditions of the people who live and work in such cities. It is fundamental that one does not consider the technical acquisitions influenced by Europe and Japan as the source of African communication practices. These technical acquisitions only constrain the cultural traditions in some ways; seldom do they actually totally replace the indigenous thinking.

Culture and politics are indispensable servants of media foundations in Africa. And while Dodson and Hachten (1973) are most correct that the modern media had been established for European convenience, the traditional patterns of African communication were the deciding influences on how media operated in modern states.

Africa's past

To appreciate the nature of the press and broadcasting in Africa, it is necessary to remember that Africans were communicating long before Europeans entered the continent; indeed, long before Arabs came to the northern part of the continent, Africans had established forms of communication. The abundance of papyrus in ancient Egypt gave rise to a culture which exploited its natural resources to record its oral traditions which existed long before the written script. Since the flora and fauna of ancient Egypt down into historic times were "much like the life now present in the southern Sudan," it is little wonder that the commerce between the lower and upper parts of Egypt, north and south respectively, was based on the interchange of cultural and social information (Wilson 1951, 10).

More recently the late Cheikh Anta Diop, wrote in *Civilisation ou Barbarie* (1983) that ancient Egyptian civilization was an African civilization with all the characteristics of the dominant black population of the continent as at present. Diop's entire thesis is based upon two assumptions: (1) the African nature of Egyptian civilization and (2) the relationship of Egypt to contiguous regions of Africa. In Diop's view, the interchange of culture and communication between the upper (Southern) Nile and the lower (Northern) Nile was natural. This is important for historical and philosophical correctness in order to assess the development of cultural values which re-appear in contemporary communication situations. As underlying myths, histories, and values govern European use of technology, so do these elements help to account for African media relationships.

ONE

Hieroglyphics were large picture signs that the Egyptians used to express their ideas. They began to use this system of writing more than seven thousand years ago (Budge 1983, 1). The Egyptians often chiseled hieroglyphics into wood and stone or wrote with a reed onto papyrus. As more and more hieroglyphics were written on the papyrus, they lost much of their pictorial character and degenerated into a series of signs called *hieratic*, an early Egyptian cursive. This form of writing was used extensively by priests to copy literary and liturgical works (Budge 1983, 7). It is not necessary here to go into any detailed discussion of the relationship of Egypt and the Egyptian language to the rest of Africa. Such work has been sufficiently done by scholars such as Cheikh Anta Diop in his *The African Origin of Civilization* and George James in *Stolen Legacy*.

Rattray's book *Ashanti* (1923) devotes a chapter to the drum language. But, while Rattray made one of the earliest European attempts to understand the nature of drum communication, he did not comprehend its wider significance. In fact, what has often not been understood is that the drum serves every purpose and function, as an institution, that writing serves. It is not clear that Rattray, one of the keenest observers in colonial service, understood this fact. The drum cannot be thought of as a single instrument or an instrument separated from the totality of village life; it is a system of communication directed and used according to the codes, rules and rituals of the society. In this respect, it is rule governed as a communicative system. It might be necessary for the drum to be used to convey messages over wide distances. This is done by one drummer relaying sound from one place to another drummer at another place, and so on, until the message reaches its destination. In the use of the drum as a medium of expression, several tones are played by the drummer that closely resemble the sounds and intonations of the language and information is thus conveyed much as if words or phrases had been amplified. In West Africa, particularly, there is a strong tradition of communication through the use of drums. Both Yoruba and Akan people find the ritual and non-ritual uses of the drum conducive to message conveyance. Indeed, it is possible to speak of a rhetoric of the drum (Asante and Appiah 1978).

THE FOUNDATIONS

Michael Appiah, of the Institute of Mass Communication at the University of Ghana, wrote a brilliant dissertation on the role of the Okyeame in traditional Akan society (Appiah 1979). Appiah's argument is that the traditional relationship of the *Okyeame* as linguist and interpreter between the king and the people constitutes an invaluable communication heritage of some African societies. Appiah is correct but did not go far enough to suggest that the *Okyeame* is the archetype of the Akan communication system and as such represents the primary mode of communication for the Akan. There are implications for media in African social contexts in Appiah's findings.

Nhiwatiwa expounded the thesis that African communication as practiced among the Shona of Zimbabwe is dependent, at the small group level, on intermediaries (Nhiwatiwa 1979). Her position is a cultural one which she demonstrates through reference to the marriage systems. When a man desires to marry a woman, he seeks an intermediary who speaks to the woman's family. This counterpart speaks to the woman's father who gives his consent for further discussions. The aim of the communicative process as practiced among the Shona people is to allow for full discussion on significant issues with as much wisdom and experience as possible (Nhiwatiwa 1979). Nhiwatiwa argues that this position is essentially different from the more direct communication model existing in Western dyads. The type of communication of which Nhiwatiwa writes is deeply rooted in Shona culture. In fact, all practices of human communication are derived from some culture base. African communication is no different.

San people and Khoisan, pejoratively referred to as Bushmen and Hottentots respectively, have left explicit paintings in caves and on the sides of rocks throughout southern Africa. Such paintings were used to record events, to illustrate boundaries, to identify themselves, and to warn others of the danger of wild animals.

AN EXAMPLE Of MOVAblE TYPE

Although the movable type was late in coming to Africa, metal and wood

ONE

blocks were used to print on fabrics and leather. This form was unique to African culture. Bronze-casting for the manufacture of a complete set of type for a printing press did not occur in Africa until the work of King Njoya of the Bamun invented the BAMUN script in 1895. It should be noted, however, that the Vai in Liberia had invented a written script long before Njoya. Others who had written scripts included the Amharas, the Benin, and many others. But Njoya, six years before any Europeans came to the Cameroons, invented his script and had the bronze-casting of the type set done so that he might print the Bamun alphabet in his book.

The book had 510 symbols, including ten numerals, in what was essentially a pictographic or ideographic representation. Njoya perfected the book over the next twenty years producing seven versions until he finally settled on the New Alphabet, consisting of seventy or eighty characters. The king had this language taught in the schools and used court and royal officials as teachers. He used the language for recording court cases, sending messages or writing laws. He had published the Complete History and Customs of the Bamun, a book which had 1190 pages, a book on religion, a book on Bamun medicine, and a map of the Bamun country. What we see, therefore, is that the first books printed in Africa were actually for the elite of the society. Thus, printing in Africa was similar in its class orientation to printing in Europe.

Both the Egyptians, before Christ, and the Bamun, after Christ, are clear examples of the technical activity on the continent of Africa in communication. And yet we have not dealt with the highly sophisticated secret cursive script of the Benin, the writing system of the Mandingo before Islam, Asante symbols of gold weights which represent an entire cosmology, or numerous other communication techniques on the continent.

pre-colonial inheritance

These examples, given from different eras and different parts of the continent show that the pre-colonial inheritance of Africans included technical orientations which were derived from Africa itself. The pre-colonial inheritance of the African communication systems takes two forms: (1) technical, and (2) political. This inheritance was reflected differentially in various regions of Africa. That is, the technical and political developments in one nation may have occurred in other years before or years afterwards. Nevertheless, throughout the continent, in almost every community, there was a technical and political orientation that was purely African, or as purely African as we can imagine, that pre-dated the arrival of Europeans.

Development of the technical orientation of communication goes back thousands of years on the continent of Africa. In fact, Harold A. Innis has shown that in ancient Egypt the concept of creation was represented by utterance and production by thought and utterance (Innis 1972, 1–22). Among the Dogon, *nommo* represented utterance, the generative power of the spoken word. Innis says of Egypt before the coming of the Arabs in 642 A.D. that "The spoken word possessed creative efficiency and the written word in the tomb perpetuated it" (Innis 1972, 13). A major part of Egyptian life was devoted to the spoken and written word. The handbooks of temple rituals developed by Thoth, the keeper of rituals, magic and formulae for Fa, were sacred, and adorned the pyramidic shrines. One of the interesting facets of Egyptian relationship to words is that no difference could be found between pictorial representations and hieroglyphic script. The antiquity of Ancient Egypt shows that already on the continent of Africa prior to the rise of writing on any other continent, the spoken word was being translated into written script. The names of kings, wars, political events and rituals were regularly written. Technical capabilities in these early times were part of the African communication context. The significance of Egypt to the rest of Africa is like the significance of Greece to the rest of Europe. From the rituals and mysteries of the Egyptian system of communication, we are able to see the dissemination of the techniques of Meroe and Axum, kingdoms which pre-date Egypt, and Egypt itself, to other parts of the continent.

Africa prior to European colonialism, was in a continental political flux. In effect, the continent was still reverberating from the massive Arab jihads of the seventh and eighth centuries. Decimated kingdoms, scattered artisans, and fragmented nations created volatile situations throughout the continent. Wars and forced migrations led to political and social instability. Yet the

ONE

strengths of kingship, a concept which emerged in Africa in the 5th or 6th millennium B.C., provided continuity amidst upheavals. From the centrality of the king to the centralization of media becomes a reality of political fact. The decentralization of economic and religious power in Western monarchies soon led to challenges of the king's right to certain privileges. However, in Africa the king was able to maintain stability and to prevent the breakdown of society. There was little leisure time to question the legitimacy of the kingship when the people were searching for stability. In this situation, the colonial experience with its concomitant slavery and settler aspects was merely an interlude in the real business of Africa. That is why we contend that the political condition of the continent prior to the colonial period is as important to our understanding of the development of media as the colonial legacy. Some African leaders have aimed for one-party states because they sincerely believe that the masses in their nations demand it, whether there is a plebiscite or not. In this sense, the political climate prior to the Europeans has affected the manner in which African governments, despite the inherited European civil systems, wield power. Hachten's observation in 1971 that ". . . negative criticism was considered irresponsible . . ." is one of the clearest points he makes in his book on African media.

NEWSPAPERS AND THE COLONIAL CONTEXT

EARLY NEWSPAPERS

THE PRESENCE of a European type printing press on the African continent dates back to 1794 in Freetown, Sierra Leone. Immediately after the delivery of the press from London, a French raiding party landed on the coast and sacked the city destroying the press, looting the businesses, raping the women, and slaughtering livestock (Barton 1979, 5). It would not be until 1800 that the Sierra Leone press would be fully operational; the same year that the press in South Africa began printing the *Capetown Gazette*. In the meantime, Egypt's press started functioning in 1799 when Napoleon occupied the country.

The publication in 1800 of the *Royal Gazette* and the *Sierra Leone Advertiser* electrified African newspaper activity. Both Africans and Europeans began setting up newspapers. Even blacks in America were to be influenced by and in turn, influence Africa. The indigenous African newspapers of this era were political and spoke out on issues related to the rights of Africans throughout the world. In fact, newspapers were seen as the most effective means of reaching the masses. Thus, Africans were galvanized toward independence and freedom by the media.

Freedom's Journal, founded in 1827 by James Russwurm and Samuel Cornish, had been the first newspaper established by Africans in America. It grew out of the desire for an independent voice for the masses of blacks in the industrial north of the United States. Russwurm migrated to Africa and revived the *Liberian Herald* in 1830. It had been founded in 1826, by a black American but closed down two years later. In a similar manner, the founding of *Imvo Zabantshndu* (*Native Opinion*) by Tendo Jabavu underscored the intention of Africans in South Africa to speak for themselves. Despite its dependence on Protestant missionaries for its initial funding it was edited and directed by Africans and became the mouth-piece for African opinion, a position it held in solitary until the founding of *UM Afrika*, the first Catholic newspaper in Zulu in 1888.

The impact of Africans in the Americas and in the British colony of Sierra Leone, where numerous freed Africans resided, was particularly significant in the development of the press in English-speaking Africa. Sierra Leone's F. A. Belgrave and W. Rainy also founded newspapers in Freetown in the 1860's. Belgrave's newspaper was called the *African Interpreter and Advocate*. Rainy's body of professionals educated at Fourah Bay and coming from various parts of the African world made Sierra Leone the hub of African journalism.

In the Gold Coast, named Ghana at independence, the *Accra Herald* started publication in 1857, two years after the founding of the African and *Sierra Leone Weekly*. Charles Bannerman, the proprietor, was the son of James Bannerman whose mother was Fanti and father Scottish. James Bannerman had been lieutenant-governor of the Gold Coast in 1850's. One of his sons, Edmund, had followed him into colonial administration; the other had founded the *Accra Herald*, later called the *West African Herald*. In 1861, Edmund Bannerman was sentenced to seven years imprisonment for embezzling public funds from the colonial magistrature. Charles did not spare words to accuse the colonial administration of out-and-out racial discrimination. He wrote, "Had he been a white man, we are certain that the governor would never had sanctioned these most extraordinary proceedings.

There is no need to multiply the proofs as to the treatment here adopted towards coloured men and white men" (Wauthier 1964, 33).

Among the leading intellectuals of the Gold Coast in the nineteenth century were J. E. Casely-Hayford who had been influenced by the brilliant philosopher, Edward Wilmont Blyden, and Atoh Ahuma, a founder of the Aborigines Rights Protection Society. Both men started newspapers. Ahuma's paper, founded in 1898, was called the *Gold Coast Aborigines*. J. E. Casely-Hayford was editor-in-chief of two newspapers, *Gold Coast Echo* and *Gold Coast Leader*. Another nineteenth century Ghananian paper was the Gold Coast *Independent* founded in Accra in 1895. A proliferation of small papers ensued as the Gold Coast readers became more literate and the colony prospered because of the cocoa production.

The missionary influence of the church press, in terms of dissemination of the Christian values, occurred irregularly throughout Africa. In some places, the church had no influence whatsoever as in the heavily Islamic regions of the Niger, Northern Nigeria, Sudan, and Mali. However, the Catholics were responsible for encouraging the press in Togo where the oldest newspaper is *Mia Holo* published in Ewe and founded in 1924. Catholic influence is also seen in the Ugandan press where *Munno*, a monthly newspaper, was founded in 1911 (Wauthier 1911, 36).

In Nigeria, the press attracted some of the leading intellectuals. Isaac Wallace Johnson edited the *Nigerian Daily Telegraph* for a while. He became the General Secretary of the African Workers' Union in 1931 and later moved to Ghana, a seat of African newspaper activity, to work with Nnamdi Azikiwe on the *African Morning Post*. Johnson became a sort of West African itinerant intellectual finally landing at home in Sierra Leone where he formed the West African Youth League.

Johnson's activity was by no means parallel with the birth of newspapers in Nigeria despite his energetic work. In 1890, the *Lagos Weekly Record* had been organized by British expatriates. By 1937, there had been 50 newspapers, operated by Africans and Europeans, registered in Nigeria.

In the French colonies where censorship was stricter than in the British colonies, it was not until the beginning of the twentieth century that

TWO

newspaper activity truly blossomed. The small readership kept the newspaper enterprise an affair of the few urban elites. As late as the 1950's *Paris Dakar*, edited by Europeans, was the leading newspaper among the French-speaking Africans. In 1920, *Le Guide* in Dahomey had been started as the first newspaper in that country but it remained a small newspaper with few readers. In the Ivory Coast, with the rise of African nationalism, *L'Eclaireur de la Cote d'Ivoire* was begun in the 1940's.

Two African nations were independent prior to 1950: Liberia and Ethiopia. Both countries were poor but had their own press. Without the technical assistance of colonial powers these nations produced their own newspapers, often poorly at first. Liberian newspapers were notorious for their lack of finished quality. Ainslie's opinion that "post-war press history in Liberia is a dreary tale" is valid on more than one level (Ainslie 1966, 71). Although she was primarily thinking in terms of press freedom, the Liberian press has struggled financially and technically as well. This is not to minimize the government's intrusion into press affairs. Charles Frederick Taylor's paper, *African Nationalist* was shut down in 1947 by President William Tubman for "libelling the President." *The Friend*, an opposition paper, failed financially because the middle class True Whig Partisans did not want to cross the government. When Sergeant Samuel Doe overthrew the True Whigs in a bloody coup in 1979, he imposed restraints on the press. Restraints that he did not place were put into effect by the papers on themselves for fear of government retaliation. Since the death of Doe in 1990 newspapers have existed under difficult conditions.

In 1956, two black Americans, David Talbot and Homer Smith, edited the *Ethiopian Herald* with a circulation of 2,000. Since the fall of Haile Selassie in 1974, the press in Ethiopia has become dominated by socialist essays, analyses, and coverage of members of the Dergue. No longer is the emperor the center of the paper, now it is the socialist doctrine. Wars among provinces and the Eritrean Revolution have dominated Ethiopian interest in news.

colonial context

When the European colonial nations divided up Africa among themselves they did so with little regard to the political wishes of the indigenous people. For nearly four hundred years of slave trading, the European nations had developed an image of Africa which was flattering to Europe. Africa was primitive; Europe was modern. Africans were inferior; Europeans were superior. Such misrepresentations of history and reality fueled Europe's desire to partition the African continent.

french colonies

The French began to form a ruling philosophy in the seventeenth century. Their methods evolved from the French belief in their cultural superiority and their acceptance of non-French who took on French culture. It was from this line of reasoning that the policy of assimilation developed (Bennett 1975, 126). All the rights of the metropolitan French accrued to those who adopted the culture. The assimilationist tendencies of French thought hindered the growth of indigenous culture in some countries.

The press in Franco-phone Africa remained an appendage of France. The reports of the colonial administrators to the metropole emphasized their ability to integrate Africans into France's *"mission culturel."* Consequently the press in Africa highlighted anthropological, artistic, and scientific investigations carried out by colonial officers, missionaries and anthropologists. French colonies were much more likely to be the avenues for anthropological or cosmological studies than other colonies. Father Placide Tempels and Marcel Griaule are only two of the numerous writers on African life in the French-speaking colonies.

Under French policy in the colonies both Griaule, who studied Bantu philosophy, and Tempels, who recorded the philosophy of the Dogon from the *griot ogotommeli*, qualified to be newspaper publishers. The French required, as a control on Africans wishing to start newspapers, that the publisher be a French citizen in good standing. This was largely interpreted to mean one who practised the Christian religion. Because of this policy,

TWO

COLONIAL ADMINISTRATIONS IN AFRICA (1914)

FRANCE	Congo, Chad, Dahomey, Gabon, Guinea, Coast, Mali, Mauritania, Niger, Togo, Morocco, Madagascar, Comoros, Algeria, Reunion, French Somaliland, Senegal, Burkina Faso
BRITAIN	Nigeria, Sierra Leone, Gambia, Ghana, Cameroon, Egypt, British Somaliland, Sudan, Kenya, Uganda, Zambia, Zimbabwe, Botswana, Malawi, Mauritius
BELGIUM	Burundi, Rwanda, Zaire
PORTUGAL	Angola, Mozambique, Portuguese Guinea
GERMANY	Namibia, Tanganyika, Zanzibar
SPAIN	Spanish Sahara, Equatorial Guinea
ITALY	Libya, Eritrea, Italian Somaliland
FREE AND INDEPENDENT	Ethiopia, Liberia

Africans rarely and only with the approval of the French government attained the proper credentials to begin a newspaper. When one considers the fact that the English-speaking nations of Africa out-distance the French speaking ones in media development even now, it is clearly a case of the French restraining the colonial subject. In those nations where there is more than one daily newspaper, it is a result of French control of those papers from the 19th century. A case in point is Mauritius. There are at least twelve dailies in Mauritius but six of them were established by the French prior to independence and three of them are Chinese newspapers which cater to the large Chinese merchant community. Thus, Mauritius is an exception in

Francophone Africa only because of the heavy involvement of French colonials before independence and the reluctance of French residents to leave the island. The French policy of transferring the locus of discussion to Paris militated against a healthy press in the colonies. Thus, as late as 1980, there were nine nations in Africa without a daily press and six of them were French-speaking. True, there may have been other factors contributing to the lack of press development in the French colonies but it is quite certain that the aim of the French government was to focus all intellectual activity in Paris. Consequently, the government imposed harsh taxes on the importation of newsprint into the colonies (Ainslie 1966, 130). This was one measure the metropole used to curtail the flourishing of newspapers in the colonies. Despite the negative efforts of government a few individuals established newspapers in the colonies soon after the Berlin Conference of 1884–85 which partitioned Africa among European powers. In 1885, *Le Reveil du Senegalais* was founded in Dakar; a year later *Le Petit Senegalais* was set up in St. Louis. By 1896, when the industrious Raymond d'Auraic started *L'Union Africaine*, the French colonies were beginning to have a number of papers produced by Frenchmen for Frenchmen in Africa. They did not seek or encourage African readers. Some of the early papers specifically wanted a Paris readership. In fact, *L'Eveil des Camerounais*, ancestor of the Cameroon's current daily *La Presse du Cameroon*, was founded in 1920 to circulate for French traders and civil servants. About the same time in Dahomey (now Benin) *La Voix du Dahomey*, *Le Cri Negre* and *La Phare du Dahomey*, the latter two papers owned and operated by Africans attempted to counteract the trend of newspapers to be published for whites only. The two Dahomean newspapers owned by Africans, *Le Cri Negre* and *La Phare du Dahomey* engaged in a persistent campaign to reveal the plight of the masses under colonial domination. Often harassed by the French officials the two papers succeeded in establishing a tradition for other Franco-phone African colonies to follow.

The first African elections to the French Parliament were held in 1932. In Senegal, at that time, the administrative seat of French influence in Africa,

TWO

a seat of hotly contested political struggle ensued between Blaise Diagne and Golandou Diouf for the parliamentary seat. Both were able candidates and both believed that the people would elect them if they knew for what they stood. So Diagne founded the newspaper *La Bastille* and Diouf started two papers, one in Dakar and the other in Rufisque: *Le Periscope* and *L'Echo de Rufisdue*. These papers, while mainly political organs, stimulated the African political leadership. Blaise Diagne won the election in 1932 and went to Paris; Diouf continued with the newspaper business until his death.

Nationalist sentiment generated considerable newspaper activity in key colonies. Although *L'Independent* had been founded in 1910 in Abidjan, it was not until the 1930's that real nationalistic feelings produced an awakening in the Ivorian African community. Such stimulation can be traced to the election of Blaise Diagne to the French Parliament. Other French speaking colonies followed the nationalist lead of the Senegalese and Ivorian newspapers.

The press in Francophone North Africa remained substantially in white hands until the emergence of national resistance in the late 1940's. Actually, *La Depeche Quotidienne*, owned by the wealthy settler Henri Borgeaud, was the bulwark of settler opinion until Algerian independence. In addition to *La Depeche Quotidienne* the settlers had *L'Echo d'Alger* run by Alaine Vicomte de Serigny, a rich industrialist. Both of these papers were strictly reactionary on the question of Algerian liberation. Perhaps the most popular newspaper with the African masses of Algeria was *Alger Republicain*. It was edited by Henri Alleg. As soon as the liberation war started, the colonial officials banned the paper, arrested and then tortured Alleg because of his support of the nationalists and communists.

When the war broke out in 1954 the nationalist movement initiated numerous papers. The major ones were *Algerie Libre*, organ of the *Movement pour La Triomphe des Libertes Democratiques* (M.T.L.D.) edited by Messali Hadj; *La Republique Algerienne* associated with Ferhat Abbas' Union Democratique du Manifeste Algerien; *Liberte*, the communist paper; and *El Moudjahid* became the foundation upon which the Algerien Presse Service was built.

The Algerian struggle for independence effectively cancelled the support for the settler papers, none of them survived the Revolution, and other papers replaced them. The revolutionary papers became the major papers and new progressive publications like *Revolution Africaine* emerged out of the joy of victory. *Revolution Africaine* started in 1963 as a voice of African revolution with bureaus in Paris, London, and Dar-es-Salaam. The Black power and nationalist movements in the United States were frequently featured as the paper tried to forge an international revolutionary front of African peoples. Jacques Verges, the editor, could not generate the enthusiasm he wanted for the paper in Algiers and moved to Paris. The Algerian version of the paper became a national paper, greatly reducing its international content.

Tunisia's press is firmly in the hands of the government. The two major papers are *La Presse* and *L'Action*. *La Presse* is owned by the government; *L'Action* is owned by the leading political party. These papers have always been pro-Arab and have voiced government policy on most domestic and international issues.

british colonies

The British ranked second to the French in territory. By 1950 the British possessions were Sierra Leone, Gambia, Ghana, Nigeria, Togo, Cameroons, Egypt, British Somaliland, Sudan, Kenya, Tanganyika, Zanzibar, Uganda, Botswana, Basutoland, Swaziland, Zambia, Zimbabwe, Malawi, and Mauritius.

The British philosophy was basically indirect rule or association; the British policy of superiority over the indigenous people did not lead to thinking that they were equal to the British even if they adopted the culture. Frederick D'Lugard explained this policy in his book, *The Dual Mandate*, published in 1922. Lugard, who was the principal British administrator in Nigeria, felt that the Hausa-Fulani Empire of Northern Nigeria was best left alone. The basic political structure of the society was efficient and stable. So Lugard's position was to allow Africans to be directly served by their own traditional administrators who would interpret the British rule to their subjects. There were, of course, inherent contradictions in this policy. The real rulers remained the British. They removed or killed intractable traditional rulers who were not amenable to British leadership. Nevertheless, the British believed in their policy of indirect rule as a guide for colonization and tried to extend it through the empire. Wilcox's comment that some territories were more fortunate than others is understandable yet, as he also seemed to know, the British colonies were fortunate precisely because there was little direct involvement on the part of the British (Wilcox 1975, 6–7).

Wilcox is a bit anxious to insist that "native newspapers often were allowed vigorous, sometimes strident criticism of colonial policies" (Wilcox 1975, 6). This is an overstatement which is aptly corrected by the statement of O. S. Coker, the noted Nigerian journalist who said, "There was very little criticism of the government" (Coker 1968, 43). There is no doubt that there were criticisms of the colonial administrations by the indigenous press but such criticism usually landed the editors in trouble with the authorities. When the entire colonial structure, from top to bottom, was managed by the governor and his officers, there was precious little freedom for African journalists to criticize the administration about their affairs. Under the guise of biblical analysis, many Africans were able to write for missionary newspapers such as *Iwe Irohin*, founded in 1859 by Reverend Henry Townsend in Nigeria. A devout church missionary society-type, Townsend believed that the African should be able to write for his/her own newspaper, and to read it. In effect, the missionaries brought the idea of a modern press to much of West Africa and *Iwe Irohin* was the first indigenous press of Nigeria. The story was much different in East and Southern Africa where English and Dutch settlers came to stay. In those regions, the indigenous people were terribly oppressed and criticism of the settler colony had to be stifled by the government.

belgian colonies

The Belgians possessed Zaire (formerly the Belgian Congo), a vast territory of 900,000 square miles and Rwanda and Burundi. King Leopold took the land as his possession in the name of the Belgians. As potentate of the Congo, Leopold invested a huge amount of his personal fortune in the colony. The colony never achieved fiscal stability and between 1887 and

1895, the Belgian government sank important loans in the territory. Part of the fiscal disaster can be attributed to Leopold's absolute rule of the territory which led to him giving some of his friends control over the ivory and rubber. Thus, large areas of the territory became private domains for commercial enterprises. But the horrors perpetrated by Europeans on Africans caused Roger Casement and E. D. Morel to publicize the atrocities of the Belgians to an appalled world in 1904 (Bennett 1975, 160).

In 1908, the territory passed from Leopold's direct rule to the Belgian government. The following year Leopold died and the colonial administration assumed a paternalistic model of direct rule. Within this system, Africans were never allowed to succeed beyond the limits established by the whites. Every aspect of the Africans' lives was controlled and directed by the Belgians. The development of the media was no exception.

PORTUGUESE COLONIES

The Portuguese controlled Angola, Mozambique and Portuguese Guinea. What the Portuguese espoused was the ultimate assimilation of the Africans into a Portuguese nation with equal rights for all those who accepted the Portuguese culture and language. Yet Portugal was even less capable of developing its policy than other European nations. It was poor, undereducated and militarily weak. And as Bennett intimates the Portuguese doctrine of assimilation was open to considerable doubt because of their preventing the few Africans who did manage to overcome all of the obstacles to gaining a Portuguese education from advancement (Bennett 1975, 162). In effect, the overwhelming majority of the Portuguese colonial populations were left untouched by the doctrine of assimilation.

Portuguese policy was most blatant in Mozambique. After establishing several permanent settlements in the sixteenth century, the Portuguese were in no hurry to set up any newspapers locally, either for the settlers or the indigenous people. In 1918, the first Portuguese language newspaper, *O Brado Africano*, was begun. This paper was not meant for the indigenous population yet it was criticized by the authorities for its political views. *O Brado Africano* had been started by a group calling itself *Associacao Africano*

TWO

and when censorship was imposed in 1933, the paper ceased being effective even for the white settlers to whom it was directed.

In 1905, there had been an English newspaper *Lorenco Marques Guardian* started for the benefit of the professionals and traders engaged in business with Rhodesia and South Africa. This paper was rather distinct from the later Portuguese papers and catered to the ruling class who understood the language of business. English had become in Mozambique much like French in Czarist Russia. Even Barton admits that the paper was "insular, self-centered and arrogant" (Bennett 1975, 160). When this paper was purchased in 1956 by the catholic Archbishop and renamed *Diario*, some had hoped for relief from its insularity and prejudice. However, under the Archbishop, it was considered the "hand of God" and it slung reactionary and racist commentary against anyone who dared believe in majority rule for Mozambique.

In Mozambique's second city, Beira, *A Voz Africana* was begun in 1932. It was the first newspaper to have an African editor. Supported by the Bishop of Beira, this paper appealed to the indigenous people to study and excel. It was the principal means by which the newly found black urbanized classes received world news.

More conservative newspapers than liberal ones were started by the Portuguese but there were the *Diario de Mocambique* and the *Tribuna*, two outstanding multi-racial and liberal voices. The *Tribuna*, founded in 1962 when revolution was eminent, was the first Portuguese newspaper to pay all writers the same fee.

Two older and conservative papers, *Noticias da Beira*, founded in 1924 and *A Voz de Mocambique*, created for whites born in Mozambique, despised the African struggle for independence, ridiculing the possibility, and pledging to fight against it.

On historic June 25, 1975, when Frelimo came to power and Samora Machel, leader of the revolution, marched into Lorenco Marques and renamed it Maputo, the fate of the conservative newspaper was sealed. At an information seminar in Macomia, Frelimo outlined its policies on the media, taking a strong socialist line. Since 90% of the Mozambican people were illiterate, the print media was not a priority. The emphasis would be on radio and a new form of communication for African villages, i.e., Chinese-style big posters. These posters would create information centers in the villages and aid literacy.

Thus, the history of Mozambique shows that the Portuguese colonial doctrine did not bring a democratic press to Mozambique. It created a small black assimilated group but left the masses untouched. The Revolution, at least, hoped to expand the pool of people who were well read and capable of being journalists.

spain, italy and germany

The techniques of the Spanish, Italian, and German colonial powers were combinations of those used by the larger and more successful colonial powers. One underlying principle seemed to have guided all Europeans in their dealings with Africans. All Africans with the exception of those in Liberia and Ethiopia had been deprived of the right to manage their own affairs by the time of the First European World War. Africans were ruled by outsiders who dictated the components of their culture that were allowable under colonial rule. Spain, Italy, and Germany participated in the suppression of culture and communication in their colonies to the same degree as the other powers.

functions of the colonial press

The colonial press served two principal functions in Africa. First, it provided the settler community with news of the metropolitan base. Secondly, it gave the settlers a sense of cohesion by reporting on the events, personalities, and activities of the colony. Neither of those functions took account of the African populations whose communication systems continued to be traditional in method and village in scope. Occasionally, through some major religious figure or unifying chief, news of the whole nation was disseminated. But the early European papers in Africa, whether Portuguese, French or British, were decidedly in the interests of the whites.

TWO

NEWS OF THE METROPOLE

A preponderance of political and entertainment news appeared in the early newspapers in the colonies. The settlers or colonial administrators wanted to read about polo, dances, theater happenings, and political events in their homeland. They remained European in outlook despite the fact that many of the early colonial administrators hardly knew any other society.

The real world was the metropole. After all, the colonials were only arms of their government and civilization. One way to overcome the enormous loneliness of Africa was for them to read about what the latest developments in politics or fashion in clothing were in London or Paris.

NEWS OF THE COLONY

This did not imply news about the indigenous people of the colony. What the colonials read in their newspapers were stories of promotions, transfers, births to colonial personnel, deaths, and other service news. Nothing occurred in the press to indicate that there were people other than the colonial administrators in the territory. The desires and wishes of the African people in social, cultural, economic, or political terms were simply ignored. The non-existence of African stories in the early newspapers was appalling. In the old *Rhodesian Herald* not until the 1950's did the editor hint at the possibility that Africans, among whom the whites lived, existed and had ideas and problems of their own.

Such disregard for the indigenous populations was endemic to the colonial press throughout Africa. Yet, it is clear that the British practised the same omission of the local people from the press in India as in Africa.

It is not difficult to believe that the press under all colonial administrations emphasized only those items of interest to the administrators and not the colonized people. In fact, the press in Ghana was just as parochial as the press in Zimbabwe (Rhodesia). News of the metropole, in both cases, London, dominated the external reports while news of the expatriates' exploits occupied the principal place in internal affairs. For all practical and journalistic purposes, Africa and Africans did not exist. This type of reporting could occur although the colonial administrators lived and worked among Africans. The *Herald* in Rhodesia was typical but by no means was it alone in its disregard of the African population.

The Portuguese were among the worst offenders. Of the nearly eleven million Africans in the combined Portuguese African territories only 75,000 had been assimilated by the 1960's. Portuguese newspapers in the colonies did not advertise the process of assimilation as desirable for the Africans and the press had little information of interest to Africans. Events considered major by African standards such as the installation of a king, the birth of an heir, the lack of rain and the presence of some spirit medium were never covered by the press. It could be argued that few Africans possessed the literacy in Portuguese necessary to be able to read the paper. Of course, the colonial authorities did not cater to the literacy needs of the masses beyond elementary conversation needed for understanding commands.

A large part of the content in Portuguese newspapers, particularly in Angola and Mozambique, the largest of the three Portuguese colonies, had to do with the statements and activities of government officials. Wilcox says that the disregard of the Africans in the press was not naivete or oversight but natural inasmuch as the Europeans were literate in their languages and owned radios (Wilcox 1975, 4). In Algeria and Tunisia, the French employed the same strategies of avoiding the indigenous African populations and speaking to the French expatriates. Wilcox apparently agrees with James S. Coleman's assessment that the media of communication among other colonial institutions were "concerned with rationalizing, perpetuating, and fostering loyalty or conformity to the colonial regime" (Coleman 1960, 334). However, it is clear that most of the rationalizations were also meant for the colonial administrators. In an indirect way, the African populations received from the colonial officials the doctrines of their respective colonial metropoles.

According to Lawrence Vambe, former editor of Africa News Service in the British colony of Rhodesia, "the aim of the colonial press was to deny the African's existence except in cases of violence against whites. It never did speak directly to Africans as equals" (Vambe 1981). Indeed, the colonial press

TWO

followed the ideological position of the ruling country. In every case, that ideology expounded the domination of the African by the European through exploitation, physical abuse and cultural suicide.

The periods of colonial rule in Africa constitute an era of persistent media propaganda against the culture of Africa. The first half of the twentieth century saw the most sustained efforts against the people of Africa in the press.

MAINTENANCE OF ECONOMIC DOMINATION

European control of the colonial media was dictated by the concomitant white control of the economy. Few Africans could afford to import the necessary equipment for printing newspapers or setting up radio stations. The Europeans kept the salaries of the Africans disproportionately low, thus allowing them little access to the capital for media acquisition or expansion. Fred Omu, writing in the *Journal of African History* on "The Dilemma of Press Freedom in Colonial Africa: the West Africa Example" says that the British chief officer in 1862 called newspapers and the freedom of the press dangerous in the hands of "semi-civilized negroes" (Omu 1968, 280).

The European philosophy, almost everywhere uniform, expounded a theory of black emotionalism, excitability and instability. Therefore, press rights could not be extended freely to Africans lest they inflame the barbaric sentiments of their fellows and cause uprisings against the colonial powers. Such were the sentiments of the British, French, Belgians, and Portuguese. In fact, in 1909, the Seditious Offenses Bill introduced by the British to control the expression of press liberty among Africans, curtailed publications designed "to inflame an excitable and ignorant populace . . . ." (Omu 1968, 243). Any attempt to inform the African population of its rights and its reasons for protest was systematically attacked as radical and destructive. The freedom of press so adamantly held to by the Europeans for themselves was denied persistently to the Africans who did, through enormous financial sacrifices, succeed in obtaining printing equipment (Wilcox 1975, 5).

As the political and economic overseers of the African continent, the European colonial administrators maintained an iron grip on the major western institutions imposed on African society including the media. Indeed, the first people given the right to collect the pennies of Africans for newspapers were white publishers who developed special newspapers for blacks. These early newspapers, controlled economically by Europeans, catered to a black readership but often in the crudest manner. Their insistence on projecting Europe as ideal and Africa as backward with no redeeming value became the instrument for the social separation of Africans. Children who gained literacy through the early grades of schools, honed their skills in Bible classes, graduated to the locally run expatriate press to obtain westernization and with it civilization. London, Paris, Lisbon and Brussels became the magnets toward which the African readers were turned.

The results of these diverse but actually connected press developments may lead to the view that the expatriate press championed the cause of African liberation. Such impression is grossly misleading and has been the basis for some inadequate interpretations of the rise of the press in Africa. For example, Hachten writes that the expatriate press was subjected to harsh and arbitrary controls by colonial officials (Hachten 1970, 25). There is no evidence of wide-spread suppression of the expatriate press in Africa. To the contrary, the expatriate press supported the colonial regimes, disseminated the colonial doctrine and upheld the missionary infiltration of the people's culture. Like the official colonial press the private colonial press believed in the inferiority of Africans and expounded the principles of the European cultural mission. So strong was the European's belief in their mission that they would often strangle themselves journalistically in order to deny the African a place in the sun. Windrich (1981) shows that the press of Rhodesia was both controlled and censored. The idea, as Windrich sees it, was for the government to completely dominate access to and content of the media. Africans had no chance to affect the media under colonial rule; they were, in effect, invisible. She contends that the Rhodesian press during the period of Unilateral Declaration of Independence (UDI) castigated the foreign press for its coverage of Rhodesia but was soon to undergo the tightening vise of the government itself. By its complicity in distorting news of Africans and its railing against the foreign journalists the colonial press had stripped itself of

TWO

supporters and legitimacy.

The African press in the former Rhodesia was under extreme pressure. Nevertheless, the African Newspaper Company, a European-owned but African-edited and oriented press, became a vital force in the lives of people in several countries under the expert direction of Lawrence Vambe. With Vambe as editor, the company published *The African Eagle* with a primarily Zambian audience; the *African Weekly* mainly directed towards Malawi, Zambia, and Zimbabwe; the *Bantu Mirror*, a Zimbabwean paper; and *Bwalo La Nyasaland*, a paper meant for Malawi.

Lawrence Vambe and Nathan Shamuyarira were significant influences on the black press. Out-maneuvering the Rhodesian government and its laws became a principal occupation of the African newspaper company.

THREE

MEDIA CONTROL AND NATIONAL DEVELOPMENT

media control

THE EXISTING pattern of multinational control of the economies of most African states contributes to the abundance of government ownership of the instruments of information. No nation wants to see its media in the hands of foreigners. Few private citizens in most African nations could afford to operate large scale media systems. In some of those societies where this is possible, there is considerable press ownership. Nigeria, for example, has a healthy record of private individual ownership of the press. The establishment in 1978 of the *National Concord* group by Chief Abiola, a wealthy businessman, indicated that Nigeria was open to private media ventures. On the other hand, no African nation permits private individual ownership of television or radio broadcasting. A considerable number of the broadcasting corporations are operated directly out of the government, while a few are operated by christian or muslim institutions.

Apart from the broadcast media there are three major types of control in Africa: i) government control, ii) private control, and iii) media trust control. Each of these types is based upon the government's philosophy of media and could not exist without government sanction. In effect, this is also the case in most countries of the world. The government, acting on the basis of its philosophy of media or its constitutional principles, legislates the proper role, responsibility and limits of the media.

GOVERNMENT CONTROL

Government control over the press takes three principal forms: i) control of the printing presses, ii) ownership of the newspapers, and iii) allocation of newsprint. More than half of the governments of Africa have a direct ownership of their printing facilities. Where huge financial outlays are required to amass capital equipment, it appears that the governments have stepped in to own the equipment. As in radio and television, it is so in printing presses. Nevertheless, there is some suspicion that government control of the printing presses is one way to ensure that political criticism will be curbed.

Poor nations suffer more from information hunger than rich nations. Their information and economic poverty invites government control of the printing presses. In Chad, for example, without government ownership of the printing facilities, there would be hardly any information distributed, because the nation is so poor. Consequently, the government is owner of the presses and the principal organs of media and provides information to the masses.

With the least developed industrial sector of any country in equatorial Africa, Chad does not have the capability of producing its own printing presses nor its own newsprint. However, most African nations are limited in the same way by their lack of industrial development. But, poor nations are usually also less capable of utilizing information. This has more to do with their lack of access to the information and lack of literacy than to anything else. Yet we know that a nation can be materially poor and fairly literate simultaneously, such is the case with Tanzania with a 79% literacy rate. On the other hand, Chad has a 14% literacy rate which effectively limits printed information dissemination.

Thus, the five government newspapers, *Bulletin Mensuel de Statistiques du*

MEDIA CONTROL AND NATIONAL DEVELOPMENT

Tcha, Info-tcha, Informations Economique, Journal Officiel de la Republique du Tcha, and *Tchad et Cultur* reach only a small portion of the 4,500,000 people. In fact, *Tchad et Cultur,* published eight times a year, is probably the most widely circulated paper at about 5,000 to 6,000 copies. A privately owned printing press, dependent on such a small readership, would hardly be profitable. The Chadian case is perhaps extreme, but it demonstrates why African governments may be the most efficient operators of the printing presses in such cases.

In countries where the government owns the printing presses, all sanctioned publications are printed by the government. A strong element of government control obviously inheres where the printing presses run only materials approved by the government.

ZIMBABWE PRESS: THE MEDIA TRUST EXAMPLE

In 1898, the *Rhodesia Heral* was begun as a commercial paper for the settlers. Advertisements took up half of the paper, and the front page was virtually all commercial advertisements. The character of the early newspaper could be seen from the layout style and stories from its inception. Notices appeared regarding new legislation, arrivals of other settlers, and innovative agricultural methods.

Africans seldom made it into the newspaper with the exception of gross advertisements such as "Camaroff Brothers for Kaffir meals and mealies." Such announcements were for the white settlers and not the African population. Early international news items in the *Rhodesia Heral* covered South Africa and Britain. Reuters, the British news agency, was the only agency which supplied news to the *Rhodesia Heral.*

Midway in 1898, the *Rhodesia Heral* established a daily edition with over seventy-five percent of the space used for commercial advertisements. By 1900, the front page had begun to reflect more international news although local news items were still predominant.

A feature in 1900 was the Boer War in South Africa. The British settlers who had come to Zimbabwe under the auspices of Cecil Rhodes' British

THREE

South Africa were particularly interested in the war going on between the Boers and the British to the south.

By 1920, the weekly edition of the *Rhodesia Herald*, now proudly referred to as the "oldest established newspaper in British South Africa Company's territories," had begun to run more news about Europe, but it was still principally British. In 1930, page layout was improved and some headlines were running across two columns as compared to single straight columns in the earlier papers. By now each issue averaged thirty-five news items with an editorial comment at the end.

January 3, 1930, a most memorable and significant date, the *Rhodesia Herald* entered the New Year with a cartoon showing a white man addressing a group of half-naked, caricatured Africans and captioned: "I am Captain T———'s detective. But because I'm disguised, these pigs don't know me." Gross descriptions of Africans began to appear in the *Rhodesia Herald* from this date. While earlier copy had simply ignored Africans, now the press took to them as the butt of every joke. When more serious items were covered, it was done in a derogatory fashion. Inter-ethnic clashes were highlighted as conflict between savages; mockery was made of every African custom, lifestyle or tradition.

A picture of an African rowing a boat was captioned: "A successful trip into the jungle may very easily tide him over until the next harvest." Nothing escaped the journalistic henchmen who studied ways to make Africans appear stupid.

The 1930 conflict between the Mashona and the Matabele covered a whole page. A Matabele spokesman was interviewed on the grievance of his people against the Mashona who were moving into Matebeleland for work. The interviewee was quoted as saying the Matabele wanted the Mashona out of the area because they were interfering with their wives and taking up good jobs. A headline in the November 3, 1930 *Rhodesia Herald* read, "Servants fear roving Matabele." According to the papers these "native wars" were proving to be nuisances for the police.

Another story in the *Rhodesia Herald* appeared with an illustrated picture of naked Africans dancing and was captioned: "These people are very fine dancers and also have musical instruments capable of real music." Stories like this one were often meant to encourage amateur anthropologists or to present the work of adventurers to a wider public. The articles were never directed toward the small African literate community nor were they written to show Africans in an objective light. Appealing to the most obscene attitudes within the white settler community, the newspaper stories supported the prevailing racist ideology.

In 1940, not a single story appeared in the *Rhodesia Herald* about Africans. South African news dominated the Rhodesian press that year with many stories on South African soldiers, goods and "discoveries" of new regions of natural resources. South Africa's influence grew considerably in the *Rhodesia Herald* through economic control by the Argus group and the domination of news through the South African Press Association (SAPA).

Consequently, at the time of the liberation struggle, the press was firmly lined up on the side of the white minority regime. Following the pattern of defenders of racist regimes which dominate the masses, the *Rhodesia Herald* referred to the liberation forces as "terrorists." Stories abounded in the 1970s of the number of "terrorists" killed. Much like the U.S. media's play on the Vietnam death count, the *Rhodesia Herald* kept scores as given to them by the Ian Smith regime.

Zimbabwe-Rhodesia was declared in 1979. Bishop Abel Muzorewa was elected Prime Minister. But, because his election was not democratic and the whites in effect remained in power, politically and economically, the press was even more rabidly racist than before his election. South African influence in the *Rhodesia Herald* was overwhelming in the reporting of the continuing war. Most of the media personnel were white South Africans and their perspective represented the views held by the minority white regime.

Consequently, it was only fitting for the elected government of Prime Minister Robert Mugabe to question the advisability of the nation's primary press being controlled by South African business. Immediately after independence, Dr. Nathan Shamuyarira, the former Minister of Information and Tourism, announced the creation of a Mass Media Trust. It was to be an autonomous body comprised of non-political civilians. Under the leadership of Dr. Davison Sadza, the Media Trust undertook to: a) buy out and remove South African interests from the papers, and b) remove capricious business interests from the media.

The first task required a $3,500,000 gift from the Nigerian people. The second task proved much more difficult as South African companies continued to advertise in the *Herald* and *Sunday Mail* for more than a year after the interposition of the non-political Mass Media Trust. Nevertheless, the body demonstrated that an organization one step removed from the government and comprising private citizens, much like the BBC, could exert an enormous positive influence on the media institutions without interfering with the work of the newspapers.

THE NATIONAL DEVELOPMENT ISSUE

Most nations in Africa present communication theorists with the problem of defining communication freedom and responsibility within the context of national development. While apologists for industrialized nations of the West seldom speak of the press in terms of national development even though the press has usually played an important role in their national maturity, African journalists on the other hand, are often ambivalent about the press as a supporter of national development. However, some journalists do support the idea of using the press to promote development.

Willie Musarurwa, former editor of the *Sunday Mail* in Zimbabwe, has eloquently expounded the national development view in Africa. He says:

> A new nation is like a budding tender plant. It has no established roots. It has no established social or political norms and mores to guide the minds and activities of its people, including the political leaders.

Furthermore,

> The national interest is still undeveloped, unknown, and undefined (Musarurwa, 1981).

The plea Musarurwa seems to make is based on the lack of political, social and economic definition within a developing nation. When the Belgians left Zaire, they left a nation in which no more than twenty individuals had a college education. Before they left the Portuguese dismantled the infra-structure of Mozambique as rapidly as they could, taking with them even the design of the sewage systems of Maputo. The British left the bulk of their subjects in Nigeria, Ghana, Tanzania and Gambia woefully illiterate. Consequently, the political inheritors of this collection of fiercely inadequately defined nations could not state their unalterable commitment to a concept of the press which rose parallel with the intellectual and economic development of the West.

Musarurwa, speaking of his own country, says:

> At the point of independence new states are divided nations. In the situation of our country, Zimbabwe, independence was won after a long internecine war which left bitter feelings and hatred in the hearts of some people. Forces of disunity and destruction are grappling with forces of construction and unity (Ibid.).

What Musarurwa argues can be applied to almost every modern nation in Africa. There was no concept of nation at the independence of Angola, Mozambique, Zimbabwe or Namibia. The same pattern is true for countries that were granted their independence without military struggle. They were, for the most part, aggregates of ethnic groups, left with their own specific histories but never really included into the national consciousness, in fact, such a consciousness can hardly be said to have existed. The Belgians ran the Belgian Congo as a base for raw materials. The people were only incidental to the political boundaries. At Berlin, the Europeans who divided the continent of Africa among themselves gave little attention to the historical and political affiliations of the colonized. Thus, the fact that Yoruba lived in Dahomey (now Benin) and Nigeria, respectively, made no impression with this type of political arrangement, it was considered by the colonizers best to keep a spirit of nationalism from developing. The remarkable fact is that

THREE

Africans were able in some cases to use the unions or a highly visible traditional figure as a rallying point for a national identity. It was rare that any of the countries, however, held a concept of nation at independence.

The reasoning, from the preceding line of argument, suggests that since new African governments are engaged in nation building and political integration, this delicate task requires the cooperation and participation of the press. Should the function of the press in African nations be the same as in politically integrated and industrialized nations like the United States, Britain or the Soviet Union? Answering this question, Musarurwa has come down on the side of most African political leaders:

> The Press must be different and play a different role, entailing a greater sense of responsibility. It must be sensitive and responsive to the peculiar situation that confronts it. It must be fully conscious of the national problems. It must understand them. It must be sensitive to nation-building, national interest, national unity and to political integration and the inculcation of political and social precedents that provide the ground norm for the formation of a united cohesive nation (Ibid.).
>
> Imprisoned for eleven years by the regime of Ian Smith for "agitating and protesting" against racism, exploitation, and the curtailing of African dissent, Musarurwa does not offer his opinions lightly. Yet he knows the inherent danger of sensational journalism which is "too sensitive." He believes in a delicate, " tight-rope walking journalism" for a developing Nation (Ibid.).

What is national development?

How long must journalists wait before they can criticize the policies of government? Is national development four, ten, fifteen, twenty or one hundred years? These questions plague journalists who understand the necessity for government to function without inordinate intrusions from a destructive press and yet who believe that a healthy press is the best insurance that the government will function for the people.

There can be no uniformity about this question in a continent the size of Africa. In fact, there are some journalists who say adamantly that "We are not going to tolerate a press which becomes for all eternity a mouthpiece of government or political party" (Abadoe, 1965). Ezekiel Makunike, the first director of the Zimbabwe Institute of Mass Communication, correctly assesses the qualities needed by new African journalists, "these were courage, tact, knowledge, daring, decisiveness, resourcefulness and sound judgement" (Makunike 1981, 1). However, despite the positive picture presented by both Abadoe and Makunike the continent suffers from differentials in growth. That is to say there are clear distinctions to be drawn between Zimbabwe and Chad or Nigeria and Botswana in terms of national development and also press maturity.

Nigerians have long contended that one of the principal problems facing their country is national integration. In fact, Bassey Obotette (1984, 53) says that the crisis of national unity "is closely linked to perpetuation of ethnicity." National instability as a result of ethnicity, social displacement, and media partisanship is said to be at the root of Nigeria's developmental problems. The state of journalism in Nigeria will not improve until the Nigerian journalist is mentally equipped to make personal sacrifices for national integration. Obotette (1984, 53) sees this lack of commitment to a national vision as the most pressing developmental question in the Nigerian media. He writes: "National development . . . is an on-going process and should reflect the basic human needs of the majority of the people of a nation." He is probably correct, that is, as correct as anyone else who would take a position on the national development question. But what role should the media play? One can agree that neither in Africa nor elsewhere are economic indicators the only criteria of well-being in a society but if one defines national development in a nation such as Nigeria from the viewpoint of national integration, what meaningful role should be played by the media?

The major determinants of national development issues seem to be the factors of health, education, political education and participation, and agricultural advancement. Thus, literacy, ideological orientation, and political

THREE

participation constitute real outcomes for most African governments espousing a policy of media use for national development.

The weight seems to be on the side of a pro-active media working to achieve national integration. Everett Rogers and Lucian Pye have contributed to the view that media play a major role in national development. Schramm has stated the thesis succinctly: "with adequate and effective communication, the pathways to change can be made easier and shorter" (Schramm 1964). Schramm's influence has been felt in almost every developing African nation. Changes in African communication systems are thought to correlate with other changes, such as economic and social integration. Thus, the idea of national integration as a goal of national development is consistent with this view. A pro-active media are an element in national integration, that is, they function to change the boundaries, to open up the society, and to liberalize the people.

The use of the media as agents in national development in African nations is perhaps valid at this moment in history. Nevertheless, African nations must be cautious that they do not allow Western correlations of media systems with modernity and national development to overpower their own perceptions of need. After all, media development is one more example of the Western imposition of a model for Africa. Conceptualizing the communication approach in Nigeria on the basis of the "great dichotomies" of Western thought such as modernity and tradition, agrarian and industrial, means that Obotette and other Nigerian theorists of the media have accepted the present formulation of the developmental problem. Although Obotette gives as his reason for seeing Nigeria's media in this way the earlier work of Frederick Frey and Lucian Pye, these rationalizations have never undergone close scrutiny at the policy level by Nigerians. Pye (1971) speaks of the "normal role" of the media as being "objective and free criticism" within a society. Pye's normality derives from his Western training and perspective. Nigeria's media may be more fruitfully conceived as growing out of the traditions of normality derived from the ancient states and kingdoms, or course, "modernity" brings its own bedfellows but the course of a nations's media, the purpose they serve and the objectives which are consonant to the environmental demands are determined by socio-historical and economic factors within the society itself.

Press Freedom within an African context is a subject which requires serious treatment. The Western writers who comment on press freedom in Africa usually do so in a uniquely Western way. They say things like "compared to the West" or "cannot expect Africa to develop the freedoms we have developed . . ." or "This is a luxury for Africa but not for us" and "developed over the centuries in the West." Rarely has there been a voice that has questioned the assumptions of Western freedom of the press. Rather than examine the indigenous assumptions of the African press, many writers like Wilcox (1975) prefer to put concepts into the mouths of African journalists and say that ". . . press freedom is generally seen as a luxury and not entirely possible at present. . ."

This is a jaundiced view. Doyin Aboaba Abiola, publisher of the Nigerian newspaper, *National Concord*, has argued convincingly that the Nigerian press, within the national context of Nigeria, held as much freedom as was necessary to carry out its responsibilities to the public during the military regimes of General Gowon and General Obasanjo (Aboaba 1979). She further states that the concept of freedom of the press cannot be considered apart from the traditional relationship of people to king. In most traditional African societies, there is only one chief, and as the executor of the people's authority, he embodies the loyalty of everyone. Whether we take a linear view or the curvilinear view, the objective reality of African society finds itself leaning toward the idea of journalists as supporters of the state. The question which must be asked, however, is whether or not support of the state is *de facto* evil and deleterious to the society. Furthermore, African theories are beginning to define and explain state support in ways which include criticism of the state. Among the Akan of Ghana, it is a part of traditional value systems that the chief or King submits himself periodically to the criticism of the people.

Support for the government does not mean absolute agreement with all policies of the government. The *Nigerian Daily Times* has frequently questioned the policies of Nigeria's leaders although the major shares of the

THREE

paper are government owned. It should be noted, however, that the reason for government ownership of the *Daily Times* stems from an attempt, which failed, of previous military governments to control the press. When an African newspaper voices its support for the government, it normally does so in defense of Africans controlling their own destiny and the right of the government to establish itself before it is lambasted by the press. The journalists who take this view argue that a young country can ill-afford the presentation of multiple voices all claiming to speak for the people. In a sense, the unitary nature of authority inherited from the traditional values of the society should not be fractured, according to this view. Yet they say support for the government also encompasses the courage and judiciousness to criticize policies of the government without questioning its legitimacy.

The complex questions of press freedom and national development receive different emphases in various countries depending on national histories, post colonial developments, literacy, and political orientation. However, communication policies are always affected by the social, cultural, and economic realities present in a society. In many nations of Africa, the language issue remains a primary problem in terms of the masses of the population. Thus, in Kenya, English has thoroughly colonized the society while in Cote D'Ivoire the French language is approaching the same conquest. What this means for Africa is that the quesitons of media control, press freedom, ownership of media, and policy formulation will be influenced by the various doctrines of the European nations. A resolution of this dilemma faces almost every African government. It is no easy task.

Therefore, the adequate protection of the media workers, including support for communication councils, training institutes, and freedom to inquire must become a principal policy of governments. This requires more, not less, newspapers and radio stations reaching into the countryside of the nations. While most media are concentrated in the capital areas because of the colonial histories, the time has come for African nations to undertake massive decentralization of the media institutions. Elite and urban communities have dominated the media and will probably continue to do so but there must be an openness to the possibilities of expansion for national integration.

Economic progress will always be tied to media progress and vice versa. Few African nations have comprehensive policies for media development. The time has come for this to happen in every country.

One of Africa's leading critics and theorists of the mass media, Chen Chimutengwende, formerly of the School of Journalism at Nairobi and Senior Lecturer, Zimbabwe Institute of Mass Communications says:

> The mass media have long been recognized in developing countries as essential auxiliary means of modern economic construction, social and cultural development. They are important means of social control and the social process. Their ideological and socialization functions are continually being defined and perfected in developing countries as one of the indispensable factors in the mobilization of the general population for programs of national development (Chimutengwende 1981).

Chimutengwende recognizes the importance African nations place on media. He sees the necessity for planned and guided development and believes that this is most consonant to the present conditions of those nations.

Communication research in the West has been greatly influenced by the early works of Everett Rogers, Wilbur Schramm and Kaarle Nordenstreng. Rogers, particularly, has focused attention on development and its relationship to communication. Rogers has insisted the "Newer conceptions of development imply a different and generally, wider role for communication" (Rogers 1976, 8). This conception of communication's role is correct because it recognizes the use of mass mobilization techniques for development rather than industrialization alone. African communicationists have either been convinced or have convinced themselves that this is the proper path for their nations. Katz and Wedell (1973, 3) say: "it is not surprising that the concepts of modernization and communication should have come to be connected." It is necessary to see the linkage in terms of mass mobilization for development because it has meaning only within this context. In fact, African

THREE

communicationists who favor the developmental communication perspective see three characteristics of such media:

(1) They assist in promoting government policy.
(2) They work toward national cohesion and unification.
(3) They popularize government leaders.

These functions are extremely valuable within the context of African nations. In the first place, since the majority of the people are illiterate, it is necessary that the media play an educational role in the nation. Thus, the media provides information regarding policies and procedures through radio which may not be disseminated to the public in any other manner.

National cohesion becomes paramount in the light of the political boundaries inherited from the colonial rulers. Linguistic groups who do not share the same customs, values or cosmology are often present within the same nation. The media must keep the national question foremost lest people devolve from nationalism to ethnic identifications. In many countries, a person is more likely to give his ethnic rather than national identification when questioned.

The third characteristic of developmental communication is the popularization of the national leaders. This is an important role of the media since African leaders rarely have access to public relations and image building firms, they utilize the media as a method of conveying their governance. Farayi Munyuki, Director of Ziana (Zimbabwe Inter-African News Agency) and formerly, editor of *The Herald* explained that part of the media's role in Zimbabwe was to let the masses know that the government had changed (Munyuki 1981). While this may be perceived as a miniscule concern in the West, for Zimbabwe and other African states, it is essential that the media disseminate a sense of stability by showing the activities of political leaders. The peasants in the rural areas are often unaware of the political leadership in the metropoles and have little identification with the political elites who manage the economic and political affairs of the nation. Therefore, the media, in its concern for national development, popularizes the political leaders. Certainly, there have been abuses of the media by political leaders who have used it to establish dictatorial autocratic rule while disallowing access to potential political rivals. However, the objective, in its purest form, is the establishment of stability and continuity in the minds of the people. Obviously, any abuse of such a sensitive objective would mean the creation of a puppet media with strings pulled at the discretion of the political leader, and, of course, the media dancing to the tune.

Mass mobilization of the population is at the core of planned developmental schemes. That is, the ability to move the people toward stated objectives becomes the test of the developmental program. The media, as information multipliers, have a major role to play in mobilizing the masses through information. According to Chimutengwende (1981), "unlike in industrialized Western countries, the mass media in Africa have to emphasize their educational and agitational role rather than entertainment." He is correct to see planned and guided national development as a conscious effort on the part of the government and people.

The idea that news and information are meant to assist nation building is a constant one in the nature of African nations (Thiam 1971, 3). Since linguistic and ethnic diversity are common in most African countries, government leaders often fear what they perceive as irresponsible media. Thus, developmental communication has come to mean a directed if not controlled media. This is a distinction that is rarely made by Western writers when discussing media. Some writers think of a directed and a controlled press in the same way, that is, they make no distinction between the two concepts. The reason for this, *inter alia*, is the penchant for a clean dichotomy between controlled and free media. However, the varieties of media institutions and functions cannot always be so neatly ensconced in an archetypical dichotomy.

For a nation to have a controlled media means that the philosophy, functions, operations and content are under the immediate oversight of the government. This is not the case in the majority of African nations. In most African nations the media is directed, which means that the philosophy of the media is guided by the government's developmental policies. Everett Rogers,

THREE

and *others*, contend that the effectiveness of the media depends upon the clear definition of the developmental objectives (Rogers 1976, 7–14; Mahbul 1976, 27). One of the purposes of the media becomes the clear statement of developmental objectives as well as information dissemination. In effect, the mass media in Africa are essential components in the modernization of institutions, social and economic reconstruction, and educational advancement in African nations (Lerner 1958; Shramm 1964).

RURAL NEWSPAPERS

Africa is essentially a rural continent. The area is vast and the population thinly spread. There are barely ten cities with a population of more than one million. In comparison, the United States with approximately half as many people is much more urbanized. Africa is nearly three times the size of the United States and one sees that the habitable region of Africa does not extend to its geographical boundaries. In fact, while people live in the Sahara, they are so few as to be negligible in terms of population concentrations.

The Addis Ababa Conference in 1961 set several goals for education in the continent. The conferees agreed to establish a target of universal, free and compulsory education for all children on the continent. However, the nations barely provided secondary education for thirty per cent of the children completing primary education by 1981. Of those finishing secondary education, not even twenty per cent were able to enter college (Foster 1980, 69).

Nonetheless, as Foster points out, quantitative progress has been phenomenal. At the primary level total enrollment has increased by 112%, and adjusted primary enrollments as a proportion of the relevant age group have risen from 36 to just over 50% (Foster 1980, 69). Such a leap in the total numbers of people receiving formal schooling placed a great demand on the information institutions. And since the bulk of Africans remain in the rural areas, the difficulty of reaching them with the large metropolitan dailies is enormous. When the large national dailies do reach the rural people, if they do, they are already four to seven days old in most nations.

The point has been made that it is often easier to buy a same-day Paris newspaper in Dakar than it is to obtain a copy of the local Dakar newspaper in Lingurere in the north of Senegal. And the people who live in the rural areas outside of Lingurere are outside of the circulation sphere even of four-day old newspapers.

Rural newspapers have proved to be useful when content and style are oriented to specific information and learning needs of a particular community beyond the reach of the metropolitan or provincial newspapers. According to Ansah et al., "The growth of these rural newspapers has been slow, but the very phenomenon of rural newspapers must be seen in the context of low literacy levels, wide variety of languages and the unavailability of basic infrastructures (roads, electricity, and services) in the capital" (Ansah, et al. 1981, 1).

Rural newspapers have existed periodically in Africa since the publication in Rwanda of *Kinyamateka* in 1933. Liberia, Niger, and Mali began the recent trend in rural journalism in the 1960s and 1970s as a form of self-education and information. The early newspapers were frequently mimeographed bulletins in support of literacy.

The Malian government launched *Kibaru* 1972, under the direction of the Mali National Agency of Information (ANIM) and of the daily newspaper *L'Essor*. A number of nations followed Mali's lead into rural journalism. *Game Su* was published in Togo in 1972, followed the same year by *Sengo* in Congo-Brazzaville. Table A lists the present rural newspapers in Africa.

objectives

Ansah, et al., (1981) identified seven objectives for rural newspapers in addition to the general purpose of promoting literacy (Ansah 1981, 11):

1. To ensure continual education for the rural population.
2. To keep the rural population regularly informed of local, regional and national events.
3. To provide readers with practical information to improve cultural techniques, health, economic and social conditions.

4. To encourage the habit of newspaper reading.
5. To initiate the establishment of decentralized local press and to help the rural population to learn to express itself in the press.
6. To ensure the participation of the readers in the process of economic and social development.
7. To provide an instrument for dialogue between the administration and the rural population.

The preceding objectives vary according to the needs of the rural district. In one place, the emphasis would be on decentralization of the local press and perhaps in another place, the emphasis would be on keeping the people informed of national events. In 1981, the Zimbabwe Institute of Mass Communication (ZIMCO) inaugurated the *Mudzi District News* in one of the least developed and most war-torn regions of the country as a way to encourage villagers who had never communicated to each other in print to learn to express themselves. Thus, while other objectives were satisfied, the *Mudzi District News* gave the isolated villagers an instrument for communication. The first issue was principally concerned with regional and local news with some relevant government bulletins inserted.

The case of Mudzi

Ezekiel Makunike, former director of the Zimbabwe Institute for Mass Communication (ZIMCO), initiated the production of *Mudzi District News* in response to an express need by people in the region to be brought closer to the contemporary political and social happenings in their area and the nation specifically. *Mudzi District News* was edited by Tim Nyahunzvi who used several journalist trainees to assist in creating the paper. They used a mimeograph machine to run off 2,000 typed copies which were distributed at the local rural market, the health clinic and the Chief's compound.

Since Mudzi is near the Mozambique border and quite a distance from the capital of Zimbabwe, the people knew next to nothing about the political decisions being taken in Harare. After the *Mudzi District News* came out, those who were literate in Shona, the language of the district, immediately became news disseminators. In effect, the newspaper was circulated many times by vocal repetition of content by literate readers.

financial considerations

A major problem of rural newspapers is the lack of financial viability. Someone has to pay the costs of personnel, mimeograph machines, transportation and incidentals. Almost all rural newspapers like the *Mudzi District News* are subsidized by the government or parastatal agencies. The buying power of rural Africans is limited and when coupled with the lack of a newspaper reading habits, the combination spells ruin for the would-be entrepreneur. Thus, without government support, either directly or indirectly, these rural papers would see an early demise. Ansah et al. (1981) are correct when they state that, "In order to bring the cost of the paper down to a reasonable level it must have a large circulation." We would add that the paper needs a "large paid circulation" in order to be self-supporting. Nevertheless, none of the rural newspapers in Africa have sufficient economic means to be self-supporting. Only one newspaper, *Elimu Haina Mwisho* of Tanzania, owns its own printing press, which incidentally was established to publish literacy materials, including the newspaper (Ansah 1981, 12).

problems and prospects

Almost all of the editors of rural newspapers in Africa are self-taught. As of 1982, only two editors of rural newspapers were trained journalists. One was the editor of *Kpodoga*, Ghana's rural newspaper published in the Ewe language; the other was editor of Zimbabwe's *Mudzi District News*, published in the Shona language. Among the more salient reasons for this lack of formal journalism training is that most papers originated with government ministries interested in literacy rather than in institutes of journalism (Ansah 1981, 30). Furthermore, the number of trained journalists in Africa is extremely miniscule in spite of the growing numbers of training institutes. There are now approximately twenty-seven institutes for the teaching of mass communication although few of them teach courses in rural journalism.

THREE

Consequently, the editorial staffs remain relatively unsophisticated in modern communication techniques. Their own on-the-job training means that the rural areas, which require considerable skills from journalists, are primarily dependent on novices. In the case of Zimbabwe's *Mudzi District News*, the editor and reporters had either completed or were completing training in journalism. The editor of *Kpodoga* holds a degree in journalism from Ghana Institute for Journalism. Ansah reports that most of the editors for African rural newspapers are "officers of extension services, school teachers, cultural animators, social workers and rural developmental agents . . ." (Ansah 1981, 30).

International assistance from foreign governments or international agencies is a feature of many of the rural newspapers. While none of them is independent of direct or indirect funds from their governments, more than half of the papers receive some international assistance. Benin, for example, received aid from Switzerland to aid the National Committee of the Rural Press in its establishment of *Kparo, Eunbuke, Imbole* and *Mi Be Nu* printed in the languages of Bariba, Adja, Yoruba and Fon respectively. The purpose of these papers was to encourage literacy retention, further education and social, economic and political mobilization of the rural people.

In the Central African Republic, UNESCO and the United Nations Development Programme (UNDP) engaged in training communicators in 1976. after the United Nations aid, *Linga*, published in the local language *Sango*, was launched. The Congo acquired French assistance to set up *Sengo* in 1972 while Kenya received aid from the Netherlands to begin *Bumanyati*, a mobile communication laboratory in which a rural paper is produced. The Kenyan Micro-publishing Unit or micro-pu as it is called, utilized six information officers trained in the Netherlands. UNESCO and UNDP have been involved in Rwanda, Tanzania, Mozambique, Angola, Zimbabwe and Zambia.

Tanzania's *Elimu Haina Mwisho* (Education Has No End) is the largest circulating paper in East Africa. It has a circulation of over 100,000 and represents one of the more effective examples of rural journalism assisted by UNDP and UNESCO. The Tanzanian literacy rate is one of the highest in

Africa and this contributes to its large readership.

The aim of most of these papers continues to be the retention of literacy. In Tanzania, the state has achieved a high literacy rate, nearly 80% literacy, yet without anything to read, most people slip back into semi-literacy. Because of this, the African nations which have begun rural newspapers, have argued convincingly that the majority of the people live in the rural areas and the greatest illiteracy is in the rural areas. Therefore, a strong and compelling need exists for rural newspapers.

Several African nations even have ministries for literacy. In actuality, both the Central African Republic and Congo maintain such ministries. In the Central African Republic, it is called in translation the Ministry of Functional Literacy, and in Congo, the Ministry of Permanent Education and Literacy. Togo, on the other hand, has a Department of Functional Literacy. Inasmuch as the continent has an enormous literacy development challenge, these special ministries and departments appear to be quite logical. However, rural journalism is not restricted to such ministries. One finds that newspapers devoted to rural populations have been initiated into ministries of rural development, information, education, national languages and health and social services. In each case the nation seeks to place the operation of the rural press in an agency or a department which is most rational in terms of national development. Ultimately, it seems that the aim of the rural press is to create literacy, maintain and advance education, encourage national integration and cohesion and develop a rural population more productive and capable. African journalists have undertaken this important task and the founding of more rural newspapers is sure to occur as the pressure to overcome terrain, literacy problems, infrastructures, economic deprivations and ethnic restrictions is increased.

The rural newspapers are plagued by the problem of trained personnel. Without minimum training, a rural newspaper just is not possible. Understanding this situation, a number of governments have moved aggressively to alleviate the lack of trained personnel by establishing schools and training institutes. These institutions are dependent either on government or in some cases church funds for their support. In the past decade, there has been a

THREE

sizable increase in the numbers of persons under training for journalism. Although Nigeria and Kenya carry the bulk of the journalism training, some nations such as Zimbabwe and Mozambique are moving fast to overcome their own deficiencies. Zambia has been a major contributor to educated journalists in the Southern African region. Zimbabwean communicationists such as Ezekiel Makunike, Tim Myahunzvi, and Gerald Siwela have been associated with the Africa Literature Center at Kitwe in Zambia.

Most training institutions, however, do not emphasize rural newspapers; they are preeminently pre-occupied with developing the information cadre to operate the major newspapers, radio and television centers and news agencies. What has happened, nevertheless, is that the by-product of this training has been the creation of a resource pool capable of handling the rural newspapers. Lack of money remains the most pressing problem in getting trained personnel to the rural areas to set up newspapers. The opposite chart gives the major training in Africa as of 1983.

Rural newspapers are important in several ways for Africa. They bring to the rural people news of the government projects, provide a source of literacy training, and give the rural people an opportunity to share ideas with each other through the media. These are seen as positive characteristics for the rural newspaper. However, most of these papers, even with the trained personnel, are unable to support themselves. Their viability is a serious problem for the government bureaucracy and, of course, to the people who depend upon such papers as the *Elimu Haina Mwisho* and *Kpodoga*.

TRAdiTioNAl MEdiA

Africa has a repertory of traditional or folk media which have always played a significant role in providing information, entertainment and national cohesion. By traditional media we mean forms of message transmission which are rooted in the culture of a particular people. For this reason, folk media is sometimes used interchangeably with traditional media. Although Western entertainment media have challenged the supremacy of folk media, they have not displaced the value of these media for the vast majority of Africans. It is possible that in some settings novelty is a greater attraction than familiarity.

MAJOR AFRICAN MEDIA TRAINING INSTITUTIONS, 1991

Ecole Superieure Internationale de Journalisme	Yaounde, Cameroon
Ghana Institute of Journalism	Accra, Ghana
National Film and Television Institute	Accra, Ghana
School of Communication Studies, University of Ghana	Legon, Ghana
Institute of Mass Communication	Nairobi, Kenya
Communications Training Center, All Africa Conference of Churches	Nairobi, Kenya
School of Journalism, University of Nairobi	Nairobi, Kenya
Institute of Mass Communication, University of Liberia	Monrovia, Liberia
Institute of Journalism and Film	Maputo, Mozambique
Centre de Formation aux Techniques de l'Information	Niamey, Niger
Institute des Sciences et Techniques de l'Information, Université Nationale du Zaire	Kinshasa, Zaire
Africa Literature Center	Kitwe, Zambia
Evelyn Hone College	Lusaka, Zambia
Zimbabwe Institute of Mass Communication, Mass Media Trust	Harare, Zimbabwe
Department of Mass Communication, University of Nigeria	Nsukka, Nigeria
Department of Mass Communication	Maiduguri
University of Maiduguri	Borno State, Nigeria
Department of Language Arts, University of Ibadan	Ibadan, Nigeria
Bayero University	Kano, Nigeria
Institute of Mass Communication, University of Lagos	Lagos, Nigeria
Nigerian Broadcasting Staff Training School	Lagos, Nigeria
Communication Centre, University of Khartoum	Khartoum, Sudan
School of Journalism, Cairo University	Cairo, Egypt
Department of Journalism and Mass Communication	Omdurman, Sudan
Nyegezi Institute of Journalism	Nyegezi, Tanzania
School of Journalism, Ministry of Information	Dar es Salaam, Tanzania
Advanced Press Institute	Lome, Togo
Institute of Press and Information	Tunis, Tunisia

However, throughout the continent, the emotional hold of the traditional forms constitutes an enormous source of communication power.

During the colonial era, some traditional forms of communication came under intense pressure from the administrators. In nearly every country, there are cases where the colonial officials decided that certain African practices were anti-Christian and, therefore, had to be eliminated. Janheinz Jahn, among others, points out the adaptability of Africans to the various impositions of European values (1961). A traditional dance in Zimbabwe performed by the men after the new beer has been brewed was outlawed by the British until the Africans renamed the dance "Jerusarema" and presented it to the missionaries as a celebration of the birth of Jesus. In the United States, the African drum became an illegal instrument because whites correctly thought it was being used as a means of communication. European values in interaction, appearance and behavior were used by the colonial and plantation authorities to justify the crushing of many legitimate institutions of traditional African media.

Folk forms of communication are the products of particular cultural and historical experiences. As such, they are by definition exclusive and provincial. Electronic communication channels on the other hand are inclusive and international. Although programming may tend toward regional or ethnic interests, the instrument itself is a public utility available to any person as a means of communication. Folk artists are using the electronic channels with increasing success.

In Africa as elsewhere, most of the folk communication traditions are oral and the arts are learned from the elders. There has been in the last few years a widespread emphasis on documentation of oral arts in Africa. Even so, no comprehensive catalogue of African folk arts exist. However, in the past few years much work in oral preservation has been started under the auspices of UNESCO.

Preservation of traditional media forms raises the issues of the conservation of tradition itself. African communicationists, following the developmental model proposed by most governments, see traditional media as a means of changing behaviors and modernizing economies and societies (*Opubor*,

December 20, 1981). The emphasis on traditional media for development means that certain structural characteristics of folk media must be modified to meet time restraints. In addition, the folk artists must emphasize nuances and intricacies of form rather than repetition.

Another issue which communicationists must deal with is the freedom of many African education systems which are at present often divorced from a child's immediate ecological, emotional, and economic environment. Education functions in such instance as an instrument of thorough deculturization of the African child. In traditional African societies, culture has not necessarily been linked with literacy or Western-originated education.

There have been two parallel streams, the oral tradition and the literate tradition, at most levels of African society. Almost all African nations have either inherited or adopted Western oriented educational systems which have no place for the rich educational resources available in African traditions.

An educational model which captures the folk media forms alongside the modern Western forms would provide for participatory inputs from the masses of people who would respond to the environment through singing, drama, dance and sculpture. A model like this would utilize the materials from the rural environments where most Africans live and modify them for the urban dwellers. Attributional knowledge would therefore be augmented by folk media forms. At the present time, African educational systems, following Western ones, are based on a limited urban life-experience although the majority of the people are rural.

Because of the heavy concentration of literacy and purchasing power in the large cities, the newspapers, radios and televisions are found in the urban areas. Electronic media cater to the urban middle and upper classes, those who can afford to own radios and televisions. However, the traditional media should be introduced more eagerly on the electronic media as a means to harness the best traditions used and to prepare youth in the urban centers for the task of using traditional media as instruments of change.

The employment of folk media for effectively and substantially conveying modern messages in a language and style which would be readily comprehended, will be possible only if participants of the traditional media are

THREE

utilized. These persons will understand the cultural and historical bases of the traditional media.

In Zimbabwe and Mozambique, the traditional folk media were used for political education during and after the liberating wars. Once the traditional practitioners internalized the messages of useful hygienics or agricultural practice their expression of the message in a traditional format secured widespread and sustained currency throughout the countryside. This pattern was repeated in dance and drama. When the song and dance caught on with the masses, it became a part of the community's repertoire and was repeated spontaneously and joyfully, resulting in iteration of the message.

There are three principal classes of traditional media based upon their form, content and performance-situation: *ritual, didactic,* and *functional.* Ritual media refer to ethnic dances such as the Yoruba *egungun* or the Shona *Dihne* and religious acts. Some theorists believe that this category of traditional media should be left untouched in media broadcasts because of the sacred nature of some of the forms. Didactic media are instructional forms which provide examples for farming, child-rearing, relationships, and responses to natural phenomena. Functional media refer to those forms which serve communicative purposes such as the talking drums and libatory speech.

four

ELECTRONIC BROADCASTING IN AFRICA

principal forms of Electronic broadcasting

THERE ARE two major forms of electronic journalism, radio and television. Both forms of broadcasting exist in Africa in varying degrees of development. Radio is the most widely used form of communication on the continent. There are several reasons for this including the (1) relative inexpensiveness of the medium, (2) the high level of illiteracy, (3) the high incidence of multi-language states, and (4) low personnel requirement for operation.

No communication medium is free and although radio is cheap relative to other media of mass dissemination, it is by no means without cost. The primary expenses in radio operations for African nations are in equipment and personnel. Equipment costs have proved to be one-time costs with most nations after independence as they have not invested money in equipment but once since independence. Some nations even inherited equipment from the colonial and settler governments. The most persistent problem of cost in radio operations appear to be the training and retraining of technicians.

FOUR

Given even the cost of equipment and personnel requirements for operations, radio broadcasting remains less expensive than television and over the long run can be favorably compared to newspapers in terms of cost to the subscriber.

Individuals in remote areas can buy transistor radios and listen to programs from the capital. This has done more to unify African states than anything else. It is not uncommon to see a lone person walking down a remote rural road with a hoe and a transistor radio, both instruments of survival.

The factor of literacy cannot be forgotten when assessing the relative value of radio to African nations. Many more people can hear than can read and this will probably always be so. With the highest rate of illiteracy of any continent, Africa has found the radio an invaluable instrument of information dissemination.

The high incidence of multi-lingual nations contributes to the attractiveness of radio as a mass media instrument. Unlike a newspaper which may provide three or four languages in a single edition with enormous production and possibly readership problems, radio can quite easily function in several languages. As many as three fourths of all African nations broadcast in more than one language and a few broadcast in at least three languages. Nigeria has broadcasts in more than ten languages.

Radio stations can be operated by two people. In fact, many of the liberation radio transmitters throughout southern Africa, were operated by one individual. However, at the more sophisticated level of broadcasting, there is a need for various technicians, engineers, programs, and broadcasters. Yet the personnel and administrative costs are nothing like what is required to get a daily newspaper out to 100,000 subscribers.

Television is far from ubiquitous in Africa. Former President Nyerere of Tanzania, argued that is was a luxury his nation and most African nations could ill afford. Yet, as a status technology, television has a wide appeal among African elites. Like airlines, nations believe that television goes with being a modern state.

South Africa, Egypt, Zimbabwe, Algeria, Libya, Morocco, Nigeria, and

Ghana are among the nations with the largest number of television receivers. All African nations with television own their television outlets. Unlike the newspapers where there are a few examples of private ownership, or unlike the radio where there are a few foreign-owned religious broadcasting stations, television is fundamentally controlled and directed by government in Africa. Specialized radio and private newspaper ownership represent only a small part of the African media system. Television is an expensive medium which many governments support through collecting license fees from subscribers to the service. The richer African nations tend to have longer hours of television service per day than the poorer nations. Equipment and operation costs figure in the length of on-air time, so does programming capacity. Without money, a station cannot operate either technically or programmatically. Furthermore, color television is as attractive in Africa as elsewhere and two years after independence, Zimbabwe, for example was fully geared for color (*Herald*, May 29, 1982).

An increasing number of the state-owned television stations are accepting commercial advertising although some, like Zimbabwe Broadcasting Corporation, expressing a socialist ideology contend that it would like to minimize its dependence on commercial advertisement (Kangai 1982). Thus, a nation's ideological posture is reflected in its public stance toward commercials and yet the reality is that few of these stations could remain on the air without commercial advertising. Whether capitalist or socialist-inclined, African nations are finding it difficult to pay for television without assistance. This was not the case with radio.

Radio came to Algeria in 1925, Tunisia in 1930 and Sudan in 1940 as examples. Yet these stations did not put any undue hardship on the colonial powers nor the later independent nations. On the contrary, just to take these countries, television created enormous financial burdens. Algeria was geared for television in 1956; Sudan in 1962; and Tunisia in 1966. Although Morocco developed radio and television personalities that aided its development with some carry-over to other countries, Morocco's entry into radio in 1928 did not cause the economic dislocation that television caused. There are other differences in such an equation, to be correct, but television is a costly

FOUR

proposition. Delivering programs costs is expensive in terms of equipment, personnel and energy.

THE SENEGALESE CASE

Senegal is on the western edge of the African continent. Its major city and capital, Dakar, is a highly sophisticated and cosmopolitan center which serves as a regional hub for much of French-speaking West Africa. Senegal began television broadcasting in 1965.

Senegal's television station is operated from Dakar. It is situated in a converted radio studio. A control room, a small announcer's studio and film projection and editing facilities and a few permanent sets installed against the walls comprise the station. Senegal's television studio remains the same size with the same facilities as when it was launched.

The problems of television in Senegal are the problems of the majority of states with television. The station does not possess a mobile unit. For an outside scene, the studio uses 16mm film which up to 1974 was processed in Paris (*Mass Media in an African Context* 1974, 13). In 1973, two Ampex video recorders owned by the station were often in need of repair and maintenance proved to be a difficulty. A report by UNESCO contended that:

> Yet the very limitation of facilities has been a major factor in promoting the use of television in an entirely African way that it is close to the people and without any pretention to rival the glamour of television in highly developed countries. (*Mass media in an African Context*, 1974)

Because the station did not have the proper resources, professionally or technically, it was unable to even achieve the type of programming which would have made it more appealing and instructive for the masses. Senegal is not alone in the lack of resources and professionalism in production. In Senegal the station has never achieved the minimum capacity of a good small television station.

Many of the problems experienced in Senegal could have been avoided with attention to the economic and cultural realities of Africa. The initial investment in equipment could have been modest but reasonable in terms of capability. Furthermore, if the nucleus was fundamentally sound, the station could add facilities as necessary. In Senegal, the technical problems stemmed from poor planning as much as poor technical expertise. The 50 w. transmitter which the government had located at Cap Vert covers a radius of about 22 miles but much of it is sea.

Installation of television facilities in Senegal was not based on a rational, functional criterion. In fact, most African television stations demand quite a lot of resourcefulness and ingenuity from their professional staffs because the technology is often imported from the West with the same rationale as the Western countries. This is true down to the make-up artists who have been known to use the same principles of make-up as their Western consultants. In effect, the Western technique often dominated television's style rather than the African ideal.

Television is a medium of the image more than the word. However, in Senegal the static cameras with the zoom lenses often highlighted the word more than the image. Restricted resources made this form of communication the most normal pattern of television in Senegal. In one sense, this served a purpose by allowing television to provide information and programs that appealed to the audience intellectually and emotionally. The aesthetic level where television becomes an art form in the conveyance of images, is yet to arrive in Senegal and other African nations.

Characteristics of the Electronic Media

The media and television stations in most African nations are state-owned and are operated like other administrative units of government. In a few instances, they are run by parastatal organizations which are indirectly linked to government. Three factors have contributed to this characteristic of the electronic media: (1) The high degree of illiteracy in the countries generally; (2) The unavailability of other means of entertainment and information; and (3) The belief that the electronic media are necessary for constructive

FOUR

economic and social development.

Radio and television receive their budgets from the central governments. Few countries allow commercial advertising, although, those few have a strong influence in the overall African media picture. Nations such as Nigeria, Ivory Coast, Kenya, Zimbabwe, and Senegal do have advertising on their electronic media. Technically, it is extremely difficult for most African nations to balance their electronic media budgets without having advertising money. They constantly face deficits and are drains on the national treasuries. Because the nations are usually poor, they are in worse shape financially than Western nations that have commercial advertising on their media, yet they want to guard against the consumerism that is often engendered by commercial ads in the west. These nations are caught in a bind; in one sense they are trying to maintain national integrity and keep consumerism under control by prohibiting the use of commercial ads on media, yet on the other hand, they are strapping themselves with the enormous burden of the state subsidizing broadcasting services. In either case, the nations pay dearly for their electronic broadcasting operations.

Centralization of programming and broadcasting operations in the capitals is an additional characteristic of the electronic media in Africa. Most broadcasting services emanate from the seat of government. In this way, government officials have ready access to the populace. There seems to be several other reasons for the centralization of the electronic media. For one, the most sophisticated audiences as well as the people who can afford electronic media, especially television, are mainly concentrated in the urban areas. People who live in the rural areas are at a disadvantage socially, educationally, politically, economically, and informationally compared to the people who live in the capital. In such centralized situations, the person in the rural districts rarely shares in the national power as expressed by media participation or control. The fact that in most African countries the broadcasting operation is highly centralized means that provincial or district initiatives are virtually impossible. Botswana, Senegal, and Mali have well-respected central broadcasting facilities and Mali was reported to have one of the most powerful radio transmitters in Africa, despite its relatively sparse population (Legum 1973, 655). Today, Nigeria, Kenya, and Zimbabwe have powerful transmitters.

Despite the lack of local and provincial initiative and participation such as is often encouraged in the Western media, there is a value to centralization in most African nations. National integration and cohesion have been managed more effectively from the center. Thus, uniformity of values, promotion of customs, reinforcement of nationalism as opposed to ethnicity, and the development of a broader view of one's society have been positive results in most cases.

Furthermore, with few trained personnel and technicians, it is easier to concentrate the resources of the nation in one place and to project from the center. As the nations mature with technicians and personnel, there is sure to come the plurality of centers and methods that are necessary for an effective participatory democracy. However, for the foreseeable future we believe that the majority of African nations will have a relatively centralized electronic media.

Administrative control of Electronic Media

It has already been noted that the electronic media operate from a centralized facility in most African nations. The forms of administrative structure are varied and represent to a degree, the idiosyncracies of a nation's current government, even though centralization occurs.

Some writers, namely Ainslie and Wilcox, have criticized the African governments which inherited electronic facilities from the British for not maintaining "autonomous corporations to insulate broadcasting from political pressures exerted by the political parties currently in power" (Wilcox 1975, 81). Ainslie writes:

> Nearly all changes in African broadcasting so far described tend away from the concept of broadcasting as a function independent of government, such as was envisaged by the British (though not by the French) in colonial days. The tasks of radio have emerged as so

FOUR

much part of, and essential to the policies of government, that many of the countries that inherited with independence a statutory corporation in charge of broadcasting, have legislated to bring radio—and television—back under direct ministerial control (Ainslie 1967, 174).

Wilcox states, that "relatively autonomous public corporations for radio broadcasting are non-existent" (Wilcox 1975, 81).

One does not have to be an African apologist to see that the evidence is contrary to these opinions when scrutinized in the light of history. In the first instance, the so-called "autonomous corporations" which existed during the colonial era were, in fact, representatives of the colonial administration. They existed primarily for the benefit of the colonial administration and reflected the official views of the colonial government, especially in relationship to the African masses. Although these colonial broadcasting entities did not have formal government status, they were in effect arms of the colonial powers. Their autonomy, in most cases, existed in the lack of allegiance and attention which they paid to the African communities.

Secondly, in most African nations the broadcasting facilities are state-owned and state-directed but are seldom under immediate control of government officials. Most governments use trained technicians. The minority of African governments that have tried to run broadcasting facilities have found it impractical. Instead, many governments have used parastatals or autonomous corporations to run broadcasting facilities. *Directed* rather than *controlled* influence is the basis for most African broadcasting. The governments do not seek to run these "autonomous" units but to state developmental goals in such a way as to persuade broadcasters to agree to those goals. This procedure may or may not work but it is in the best tradition of democracy. On the other hand, those nations which have used heavy-handed techniques, forcing broadcasters to follow an official line have lost a legitimate avenue for mass participation in decision making. Directing the broadcasters through persuasion and argument is far more effective in the long run than trying to control them through intimidation, fear, and torture;

methods which are not unknown in Africa.

Wilcox's "relatively autonomous public corporations" is so ambiguous as to be meaningless when one speaks of African broadcasting. Either the corporation is public or state; either it is autonomous or not; and "relatively autonomous" is like being a little pregnant in the sense that you are either so or not so.

Inasmuch as few African nations have individuals who possess the capital to control broadcasting, the majority of the nations have vested power in parastatals or public corporations which act in the interest of the public. Zimbabwe, Ghana, Kenya, Nigeria, Zaire, Liberia, Egypt, Sudan, Senegal, and Ivory Coast are a few of the nations that follow this pattern. The fact that these nations possess public corporations or parastatals does not completely insure against governmental interference. Furthermore, since funding is usually from government sources, most likely from ministries of information and telecommunication, government can be expected to scrutinize the broadcasting operations. Nevertheless, given the economic situations, the remaining paucity of trained personnel, and the developmental schemes of most nations, the broadcasting personnel in many nations do an exceedingly effective job, technically and professionally.

Electronic broadcasting by region

Western Africa

Countries in the Western region of the continent of Africa include Benin, Burkina Faso, Cape Verde, Gambia, Ghana, Guinea, Guinea-Bissau, Côte d'Ivoire, Liberia, Mali, Mauritania, Niger, Nigeria, Senegal, Sierra Leone, and Togo. Population ranges from 412,000 in Cape Verde to 122,500,000 in Nigeria. Total population of the western region is more than 250,000,000. Area for these countries ranges from 4,033 square kilometers in Cape Verde to 1,267,000 square kilometers in Niger. Total area of the region is 6,129,070 square kilometers. All governments in the region are centrally controlled. A number of them are military dictatorships with weak media systems.

FOUR

Each country transmits radio and television broadcasts except for a lack of television in Gambia. The earliest radio broadcast in the region originated in Ghana in 1935. The last West African country to initiate radio broadcasts was Gambia in 1962. Television broadcasts began in each country during the period from 1959 in Nigeria to 1965 in Senegal. The government of each country owns the broadcast facilities except for some private and religious ownership in Gambia, Sierra Leone, and Liberia. Nigerian facilities are owned by a public corporation.

CENTRAL AFRICA
Countries in the central region of the continent of Africa include Cameroon, the Central African Republic, Chad, the Congo, Equatorial Guinea, Gabon, Sao Tome and Principe, and Zaire. Population ranges from 150,000 in Sao Tome and Principe to 41,000,000 in Zaire. Total population of the central region is over 70,000,000. Area for these countries ranges from 964 square kilometers in Sao Tome to 2,344,885 square kilometers in Zaire. Total area of the region is 5,341,193 square kilometers. The governments in these countries tend to be one party governments. Recently Zaire, the Congo and Gabon have indicated a shift towards multi-parties.

Each country transmits radio and television broadcasts except Sao Tome and Principe. The earliest radio broadcast in the region originated in Congo (Brazzaville) in 1935, followed almost immediately by Zaire (Belgian Congo) in 1936. The last central African country to initiate radio broadcasts was Gabon in 1959. Television broadcasts began in each country during the period from 1963 in the Congo and Gabon to 1985 in Cameroon. In every case the government of each country owns the broadcast facilities except for some foreign private ownership in Chad and Gabon.

EASTERN AFRICA
Countries in the eastern region of the continent of Africa include Burundi, Djibouti, Ethiopia, Kenya, Rwanda, Seychelles, Somalia, Sudan, Tanzania, and Uganda. Population ranges from 66,229 in Seychelles to 40,000,000 in Sudan. Total population of this region is more than 170,000,000. Area for

these countries ranges from 454 square kilometers in Seychelles to 2,505,813 square kilometers in Sudan. Total area of the region is 6,195,090 square kilometers. The governments of this area are mostly one party administrations. Each country, with the exception of Rwanda, transmits radio and television broadcasts. The earliest radio broadcast in the region originated in Kenya in 1928. The last east African countries to initiate radio broadcasts were Rwanda and Seychelles in 1965. Television broadcasts began in each country during the period from 1962 in Kenya and Sudan to 1983 in Seychelles. The government of each country owns the broadcast facilities except for some private ownership in Somalia. Burundi and Rwanda have expressed interest in joining the International Telecommunications Satellite Orangization (Intelsat).

NORTHERN AFRICA

Countries in the northern region of the continent of Africa include Algeria, Egypt, Libya, Morocco and Tunisia. Population ranges from 6,000,000 in Libya to 57,000,000 in Egypt. Total population of the northern region is 140,000,000. Area for these countries ranges from 154,530 square kilometers in Tunisia to 2,381,741 square kilometers in Algeria. Total area of the region is 6,020,350 square kilometers. The governments of Algeria, Tunisia, Egypt and Libya are dominated by one major political party, although Egypt is considered democratic. Morocco is a monarchy.

Each country transmits radio and television broadcasts. The earliest radio broadcast in the region originated in Algeria in 1925, followed almost immediately by Egypt in 1926. The last north African country to initiate radio broadcasts was Libya in 1957. Television broadcasts began in each country during the period from 1954 in Morocco to 1966 in Tunisia. In every case the government of each country owns the broadcast facilities.

SOUTHERN AFRICA

Countries in the southern region of the continent of Africa include Angola, Botswana, the Comoro Islands, Lesotho, Madagascar, Malawi, Mauritius,

FOUR

Mozambique, Namibia, Reunion, Saint Helena, South Africa, Swaziland, Zambia, and Zimbabwe. Population ranges from 5559 in Saint Helena to 36,000,000 in South Africa. Total population of the southern region is 110,000,000. Area for these countries ranges from 122 square kilometers in Saint Helena to 1,246,700 square kilometers in Angola. Total area of the region is 6,576,538 square kilometers. The governments of Angola, Botswana, the Comoro Islands, Madagascar, Malawi, Mozambique, Zambia, and Zimbabwe are elected by the majority of the people. South Africa is a minority government. Lesotho and Swaziland are monarchies. Mauritius is socialist. Namibia is an independent democracy. Reunion is a French dependency. Saint Helena is a British dependency.

Each country transmits radio and television broadcasts except Botswana, the Comoro Islands, Lesotho, Malawi, and Saint Helena. The earliest radio broadcast in the region originated in South Africa in 1923. The last southern African country to initiate radio broadcasts was Botswana in 1972. Television broadcasts began in each country during the period from 1961 in Zambia to 1965 in Madagascar and Mauritius. In every case the government of each country owns the broadcast facilities except for some private ownership in Malawi, Mozambique, and Reunion.

SATELLITES

In 1970, King Hassan II of Morocco officially dedicated the first communications satellite earth station in Africa ("Building a Pan African Communication Network," [*Africa Report* 1972, 30]). This was the beginning of African interest in achieving total satellite coverage of the continent. Alfred Opubor, a leading communicationist in Africa, has said, "The presence of satellite communication will greatly reduce the inconvenience of communicating with someone on the other side of the continent" (Opubor 1979). No longer will cables, telex, telephones and micro-wave relays have to be oriented toward Europe once the satellite network is fully operational. Many nations already have earth stations and many more have them in their developmental plans. The more than 20 earth stations that now exist comprise a limited network.

Nigeria became a leader in telecommunications during the oil boom of the late 1970s. By 1983, it had firmly established a marisat station in Port Harcourt for ship-to-shore communications that would allow any subscriber to dial any ship from any telephone direct to passengers on board over 35 kilometers of land. In addition, Nigeria has earth stations at Lanlate and Kujama. The Kujama station is state-of-the-art technology. A massive disc (105 feet in diameter) is the most expensive single item at the terminal. Kujama is an Intelsat station with an operation from where the ultra modern antenna, special teleprinter equipment, engineering service channel facility, weather chart and order wire are located. It can communicate directly with Lanlate in Nigeria as well as with West Germany, Britain, Canada, the United States, and other African nations (*Weekly Eagle* 1983).

Such diversification of operations will help all of Africa in its distributive communication networks. A Domsat link allows a country like Nigeria to connect the southern and northern parts of the nation. International events are as efficiently handled with Intelsat and other type of satellites. Africa is slowly evolving into the communication age through the international telecommunications networks.

problems and prospects for advanced technology in Africa

As telecommunication technologies continue to foster change upon African society, the challenge to government officials becomes greater as questions continue to arise concerning development implications for the future. Lindenau (1984) calls this period of the technological revolution "the worst of times" (18). For Africa, the situation could be disastrous if the continent continues to fall behind. Without intellectual and political commitment to technological changes, Africa will be unable to cope with the demands of the future. The importance of obtaining the competence to use technology and enhance skills cannot be underestimated. Mere survival in tomorrow's high-technology information age means that a nation will have to play in the technological arena or become an obsolete icon of a past age. The challenge facing Africa is rapid preparation for communication change. This also requires a re-thinking of the present social and political goals and a remodeling of political structures. In other words, innovations in the way African nations respond to the food crises, population, and disease issues will depend on technology.

Africa can use a more open approach to the electronic revolution. There are several aspects to resistance to electronic technology which appear constant in African societies. The traditions often discourage innovative applications of new technologies. We postulate that the historical lag of the application of advanced electronic technology in Africa is due to:

1. The view that change means some uncertainty and resistance is an attempt to preserve the status quo.
2. Traditional uses of radio have become so widely available and popularly affordable that advanced technological systems seem unnecessary.
3. Some societies see advanced technology as an alien model that would introduce unwanted consequences.
4. The growth of government bureaucracies has strained the limited qualified personnel resources which would have been useful in an expanding sector of advanced technology.
5. The lag is also due to the poor economic conditions generally existing in Africa.

The impact of telecommunications technology on a society is far more extensive than we could have imagined just a few years ago. Advanced technology pervades the life of individuals in Western societies and will surely assist Africa, if it is ever able to move to an affirmative posture with regards to advanced technology. While we are aware of the economic constraints of most of the African nations we also believe that advanced technology is necessary for the African economies to expand. The principal influence in politics and economics in the next century will be telecommunications.

Africa must begin to research new technologies, interactive video, and low power broadcast. In fact, African governments should hold open dialogue on advanced technology with members of the university communities. This is not to say that Africans have been totally outside of the discussion about advanced technology but rather to emphasize the need for the continent to be more intensely involved in the process of restructuring its telecommunications. In the West it has been the academic community which has led in these areas. Thus, in Africa, an academic-government-industry relationship might be developed to address these issues. This is one way African governments might generate more research and clarity in the area of telecommunications application.

Technological Forecasting

The technological revolution or information age has stimulated new developments in research and applications. This has brought about more interest in the subject of technological forecasting as a research tool. The potential of technological forecasting was realized many years ago. According to Ayers (1969), intuitive forecasting is one technique considered to be more scientific. Intuitive forecasting is individual or group guessing to accomplish the following:

   a) ensure that everyone is focused on precisely the same question.
   b) allow for all participants to consider all aspects of future trends (technical, economic, political, social, etc.)
   c) remove pressures of personal interactions. (Pelton 1981, 178)

There are several techniques of intuitive forecasting such as the delphi and the pyramid techniques. The delphi system is essentially based on questions which are developed to ascertain when an event may occur. After several rounds of deciding what questions are most readily answerable, group consensus is produced. On the other hand, the pyramid technique is based on declarations where many people are asked to declare what they see as their needs.

FOUR

The Pyramid Technique

Africa is perhaps best situated culturally to utilize the pyramid technique which was developed out of the Video Letter Exchange Project between Senegal and the United States produced by Dhyana Ziegler in conjunction with OEF-International and the Delta Research and Educational Foundation in 1989.

The technique uses need declarations of villagers or people in urban communities as the base or substance for forecasting. Once the people have expressed their needs, the needs are transmitted to government officials and other professionals who clarify the meaning of the needs. The pyramid technique is especially important in societies where the people may not know the various functions or names of advanced technology systems.

An example of how the pyramid techniques might work was revealed in the Video Letter Exchange Project when a villager explained that the health center had been destroyed. In the pyramid technique such a need declaration would be transmitted to officials who would use the declaration as a way to clarify technological and telecommunications needs. For example, the specialists or officials may decide to install a system for communicating medical advice from the capital to the village as well as to rebuild the health center. As a forecasting method the pyramid technique would assist African governments in clarifying needs from the base to the top.

Telecommunications technology has revolutionized the potential of all societies since no generation before this one has had the capability of receiving instantaneous information. Telecommunications technologies have opened up many new doors for today, as well as challenges for tomorrow. The answer to how Africa deals with these issues and changes is not known but forecasting should play a vital role in development.

Telecommunications Technology Applicable to African Nations

There are several telecommunications technologies which are adaptable and applicable to Africa. It should be noted, however, that the following list is not inclusive of every existing technology. Nevertheless, we have included those technologies which are readily useful in Africa.

Audio and Video. Audio and video are both applicable to African society. We believe that the audio-visual medium is superior to the audio-only medium as exhibited by the Video Exchange Letter Project.

Audio-visual Overhead Projectors. The use of audio-visual overhead projectors is also a viable means of delivering information. Audio-visual overheads are used with slides or transparencies and considered a technology which is easy to use and inexpensive. Research suggests that overhead projectors are inexpensive and easy to use but can result in a tuning-out from the audience if the presenter is not familiar with the medium or does not take into account how the material should be presented.

Audio Teleconferencing. Innovations using audio have advanced where now audio-teleconferencing is as simple as a conference phone call. However, audiographic teleconferencing offers a little more flexibility because it uses voice and graphical information over standard telephone lines.

Tele-conferencing. Another telecommunications technology useful in Africa is the art of tele-conferencing. Tele-conferencing would allow people to gather at different sites where they could talk back and forth using two-way audio and video systems.

Slow Scan Video. Slow scan video is also adaptable to many societies because it has the technical capabilities of the freeze-frame which allows a participant to view one still frame image at a time. The slow scan video would allow more time for any kind of information to sink in or images to be stored in the mind.

Interactive Video. Interactive video is applicable to all teaching curriculum functions. For example, a network may be used to link four health centers or schools so that the participants can see and hear each other.

Video Cassette Recorder (VCR). The rapid growth of the video cassette recorder industry opens many opportunities for African societies. The VCR allows for convenience because a person can play a cassette tape whenever they choose. Additionally, with the VCR, a cassette tape can be played over and over again as a reinforcement to learning. This advantage of the VCR can aid retention and also serve as a convenient tool for educating people in

FOUR

distant regions of a nation.

Videodiscs. Videodiscs is another telecommunications technology with many applications. The advantage of the videodisc is that it can be produced in large quantities and at a low cost. Furthermore, the videodisc is flexible and highly storable. Videodiscs can interface with computers for individualized instruction in such a way that people are in control of the technology.

Telecourses. The production of telecourses is presently becoming a fast growing concept in Africa. In Nigeria and Kenya, professionals have begun to develop telecourses on various subjects. Colleges in Africa might develop telecourses on health, child care, literacy, and the functions of government. Telecourses usually require an experienced production team to work in conjunction with an academic team.

Cable. Cable is able to connect many facilities throughout a country. Several African nations have expressed interest in cable systems. Cable offers an instrument for distant teaching as well as a means for interconnecting communities.

Direct Broadcast Satellites. Direct Broadcast Satellites began with the 1965 launching of the first International Telecommunications Satellite Consortium (INTELSAT). Several national educational organizations became interested in DBS after an agreement was made between the U.S. National Aeronautics and Space Administration (NASA) and India for the use of the Application Technology Satellite—ATS-F (later changed to ATS-6 after launch) "to explore the social benefits of communication satellites" (Polcyn 1979–80, 156). According to K. S. Sitaram (1983), the Satellite Instruction Television Experiment (SITE project) "is the largest experiment ever done on educational television using DBS and the largest experiment of intercultural broadcasting" (p. 6). The experiment which was completed in 1976 indicates that satellites can be used to send information to different cultures. Sitaram (1982) makes the following comments about the SITE project:

> ... the Satellite Instructional Television Experiment (SITE) conducted in India in 1976 has shown that the satellite can be used to transmit information on agriculture, education, and family planning

to large numbers of people speaking several languages. (1982, 4).

Videotex and Teletext. Videotex and teletext are two other telecommunications technologies which are accessible to Africa. Teletext is basically a one-way telecommunications system and videotex is a two-way telecommunications system.

Teletext. A user goes from the information source which can be either cable or a broadcast television station, and receives a graphic display system over-the-air on the screen. Videotex—a user goes from the information source via cable or the computer to the TV set or the terminal (Video Age 1984). Mel Goldberg (1984) makes the following comments regarding teletext and videotex:

> One of the major factors in teletext or videotex is the telephone. With the telephone, teletext may become two-way. It's called hybrid by the engineers. Telephone means that people can get the information on the one-way screen but then they can call up and receive what ever they want. The phone means they have an interactive communication, and that's where the big news really will be in the future in my opinion (1984, 9).

Fiber Optics. Fiber optics is the use of light pulses carried by glass fibers in place of wire-carried electrical signals in telephonic transmissions (Thomsen 1983, 119). Fiber optics will make it easier for computers to communicate with other computers according to Thomsen (1983, 119). Therefore, as computers continue to play an integral role in the world, African nations will be forced to consider methods of integrating their electronic systems for greater efficiency.

Computers. Computers can be used for a number of skills such as mathematical functions, word processing, manipulating data in a research project, as well as the art of searching through established data bases (Howarth 1983, 125). Stonier (1982) lists some other advantages of using computers in education:

FOUR

1. The computer is interactive. Unlike books, tapes, films, radio and television, what happens next is largely determined by the user. This gives the learner a sense of personal control. In addition, by eliciting a response and involving motor activity, the pupil becomes actively engaged in the learning process.
2. A computer has infinite patience. One student remarked "it was the first math teacher who never shouted at her."
3. The computer provides privacy. Children or teachers can make mistakes without anyone seeing them. It is easy to erase and start again. Good programs never put pupils down, instead, good programs provide effective positive reinforcement.
4. A computer can provide individual tutoring and attention to a level not possible in most classroom situations (Stonier 1982, 13).

SUMMARY

Telecommunications technology will bring many challenges, innovations, and frustrations to Africa. Although the potential use of telecommunications technology has not been fully realized by some countries, it is evident that telecommunications technology will play a major role in the future. Telecommunications technology has the potential to enhance learning on many levels, speed up the delivery of education and increase productivity, and deliver health and sanitation information, but proper training is required for practitioners to explore its potential and use it effectively. However, the problems and issues surrounding the uses of telecommunications technology will have to be resolved before the merging of technology and political education can be effectively made. Social and political institutions can play a vital role in the development of policy for most African nations. Attention will have to be given to issues such as accessibility, cost, and programming.

five

TWO NATIONAL PERSPECTIVES ON THE MEDIA

Nigeria: The Turbulent Road to Unity

AFRICA'S MOST populous nation has exemplified the greatest amount of press freedom although press freedom in the Western sense has often been threatened. Fred Omu's *Press and Politics in Nigeria 1880–1937* (1978) shows that prior to independence, the foreign as well as the indigenous press in Nigeria, were subject to criticism from the British government. Obotette (1984, 93) says that most of the newspapers that the early "Nigerian elites came in contact with were political and occasional in nature."

Nigeria's modern press does not have the antiquity of the Ghanaian, Liberian, or Sierra Leone an press in West Africa but it is more richly endowed with color and controversy. Of course, the earliest paper to be published in Nigeria was the pro-colonial *Anglo African* whose name had nothing to do with the integration of the two societies. On the contrary, the *Anglo African* began publishing in Lagos in 1863 as a glorification of "ordered and civilized government" (*Daily Times* of Nigeria Ltd., Annual

FIVE

Report 1964–65). The only references to the indigenous people were derogatory, humorous, or related to domestic service. The *Anglo African* became the official instrument of the colonial territory with mainly commercial or political activities (Obotette 1984, 94). As in other cases where colonialism held sway, the aim of the colonial newspapers was to provide the colonialists with news of their expatriate society and information about the political and commercial dealings in the metropole. The *Anglo African* served the whites well during the time Robert Campbell was editor and publisher.

It was not long, however, before nationalism barely, twenty years old, led to demands for a newspaper to reflect African interests. A group of Nigerians started the *Lagos Times* and made it clear that the colonial conditions were not permanent and that the people on the west coast of Africa would one day again exercise power over their internal and external affairs (Obotette 1984, 96). Other newspapers, some with familiar orientations, were established. In one brief period, the *Lagos Observer* (1891), the *Lagos Standard* (1903), *The Chronicle* (1908), and the *Nigerian Times* (1914), blossomed and faded. Obotette has argued unpersuasively that these papers disappeared because "they were ingeniously organized" (1984, 97). That is probably one of the reasons why the papers died; yet one would think that publishers would have learned something from their predecessors. This did not seem to be the case. Actually, the most logical reason for the decline of these early indigenous papers was the inability of the small "literate-in-English" elite to sustain them financially.

Several other newspaper ventures sprang up to meet what some saw as a growing "literate in English" elite and a sizable colonial bureaucracy. In 1926, the International Paper Company which owned the London *Daily Mirror* came to Nigeria and began the *Daily Times*. The aim of the International Paper Company was to provide news that could be readily consumed by the growing African elite class while maintaining a majority white leadership.

Duse Mohammad Ali, an Egyptian with strong Pan-African sentiments, took up residency in Lagos and began publishing his newspaper, *The Comet*. Ali had been associated with W. E. B. Du Bois and Sylvester Williams during the Pan-American conferences held in London and had decided to start a paper in the country which he thought held the key to the future of Africa. Accordingly, *The Comet* was essentially meant to bring the Nigerian readers into the mainstream of world opinion. The purpose of *The Comet* as Ali and his editors saw it was to "deal with larger issues affecting West Africa rather than minor issues of Nigerian Politics" (Ezera 1964). Such a position allowed Ali to stay clear of the British in Nigeria, the place of his business, while attacking them in the Gold Coast or Gambia. Furthermore, Nigerian politics, whether of a nationalistic or colonialistic nature, was not to embroil *The Comet*.

Missionary influence on the indigenous societies of Africa was severe; such was the case in Nigeria with regard to the media. As secular organizations and individuals, from within and from outside the country, established newspapers, the Christian missionaries jumped into the race. Such newspapers as *Leisure Hours,* (1917); *African Hope,* (1925); *African Church Gleaner,* (1925); *Nigerian Methodist,* (1925); *African Christian,* (1931); *Church Chronicle,* (1934); *Nigerian Mail,* (1935); *Unwana* and *Obodom Edem Usiak Utin* in (1935); and *Christian Life* in (1936), were established by various church groups and appeared weekly or when they were ready for distribution (Obotette 1984, 97).

In the background to the drama being played out on the Nigerian field, hovered the Church's intention of winning as many people as possible into its fold. Thus, the establishment of newspapers was seen as one of the best ways to increase the readership of the Bible thereby assuring the Church of ready access to the literate elite. Most of these publications, however, suffered in comparison with the secular newspapers because they seldom had outside news and rarely ever gave the African reader a point of view about the colonial situation. Thus, although there were missionary papers, they could not quench the insatiable thirst for political and worldly information that seemed to grip the Nigerian.

In 1921, Herbert Macauley had begun his *Lagos Daily News* as the main organ for the dissemination of his political views. He founded the Nigerian Democratic Party and effectively used the *Lagos Daily News* for political and

FIVE

social education. Macauley's contributions to the national consciousness of Nigeria through his newspaper is one of the early stories of the media's influence in Nigeria. Other newspapers with mainly a political agenda followed Macauley's lead. Numerous newspapers have contributed to the political consciousness of Nigerians, including but not limited to, *Iwe Irohin*, *West African Pilot*, *The Daily Service*, *Northern Advocate*, *Gaskikya Ta Fi Kwabo*. The flavor of these papers can be gathered from a comment by Obotette:

> The pre-independence newspaper might have been used to fan an air of nationalism by attacking imperialism, but they were not untouched by internal political rivalries among tribal leaders. They were purely political and oppositional. The language, too, was abrasive and provocative—with total disrespect for office and persons (1984, 100).

Obotette's judgement is in line with the view held by Omu (1978). Apparently the jockeying for political position and posture during the pre-independence years meant that politicians in control of the newspapers felt the necessity to knock their opponents out of contention for leadership roles. Whatever the case, the result was a highly politicized population, one frequently polarized along ethnic lines.

The caustic language often found in current Nigerian newspapers when attacking a rival or opposition political party is considered fair. Numerous politicians have felt the sting of some sharp tongued Nigerian editor, most often of the opposing political camp. In fact, the intemperate language employed in the press does not seem to change whether the sitting government is civilian or military (Aboaba 1979). In a study of the Nigerian press under military rule, Doyin Aboaba discovered that the conditions for press freedom were equally as available for Nigerian journalists whether during military or civilian governments. In effect, what she measured was whether or not journalists were permitted to attack policies and personages of the administrations without retaliatory action being taken.

Nigeria's newspapers have inherited a history of oppositional squabbles

MAJOR NIGERIAN NEWSPAPERS, 1990

Newspaper	Place of Publication	Estimated Circulation	Affiliation
Daily Sketch	Ibadan	75,000	Owned by Ogun, Oyo and Ondo States
Daily Star	Enugu	75,000	Owned by Anambra State
Daily Times	Lagos	400,000	60% owned by federal government
The Mail	Lagos	50,000	Privately owned
National Concord	Lagos	150,000	Privately owned
New Nigerian	Kaduna	80,000	Owned by federal government
Nigerian Herald	Ilorin	100,000	Owned by Kwara State
Nigerian Statesman	Owerri	50,000	Owned by Imo State
Nigerian Tide	Port Harcourt	50,000	Owned by Rivers State
Nigerian Tribune	Ibadan	96,000	Privately owned
The Nigerian Chronicle	Calabar	80,000	Owned by Cross River State
The Guardian	Lagos	150,000	Privately owned
The Nigerian Observer	Benin City	150,000	Owned by Bendel State
The Punch	Lagos	150,000	Privately owned

and intellectual debate which has not been all bad for the nation, though this history has taken its toll on some good journalists and politicians. We shall now turn our attention to specific issues confronting the media in Nigeria.

Aboaba (1979, 107) writes about the Nigerian press as follows:

FIVE

Historically, the Press served as a unifying force in two major, collective, emergency experiences: Nigerian independence and the civil war. Thus, the press responded to the problem of its proper role in normal times in the administration of the country partly because of its eagerness to adopt Western concepts and theories and partly because of the complex nature of its situation in a multi-ethnic, developing country.

She sees a developmental function in the press' attitude toward independence and civil war. After all, in a diverse, multi-ethnic society, the press is needed for national cohesion. Again the "unifying element" occurs in the discussion of the press' significance. Obotette (1984, 113) says "The desire to establish mass media that would insure national unity has become a common concern in Nigeria." Although Obotette believes that the initial development of media in Nigeria was essentially along ethnic and regional lines, he is certain that there is a new trend among journalists. It is evident that regional antagonisms still exist but they are being minimized by the increasing similarity of the economic and social problems being faced by the population. Intensification of regionalism and ethnocentrism has occurred during periods of extreme distrust, e.g., just prior to or after a military coup.

The road to national unity in Nigeria will continue to pass through the sacred forest of regional and partisan newspapers until there emerges in the future a national consensus that cuts across ethnic and regional boundaries. Television has the best chance to succeed in showing the great beauty in the country's diversity. In the attempt to forge the national will toward unity, television may play a much more positive role than the faction newspapers whose colorful and controversial histories are also a part of the freedom of press doctrine.

SOUTH AFRICA: A SPECIAL CASE OF RESTRAINT

In December, 1983, the International Press Institute of London called South Africa one of the worst offenders of the rights of journalists. The IPI report said 15 editors of South Africa's 24 major newspapers had been convicted or threatened with prosecution by a government bent on press subservience to racial separation. The IPI's membership includes 2,000 editors and publishers in 60 nations (*New York Times*, December 18, 1983). Perhaps, no country in history has arrested more journalists, closed down more newspapers, imprisoned more reporters and attempted to dictate more information than the South African government. Although the rest of Africa is not entirely free of government harassment of journalists, South Africa is in a category alone in terms of press restrictions and threats.

There is a record of government harassment of journalists in Africa. This is largely due to several rather repressive regimes led by South Africa rather than to any continent wide oppression of media personnel. The South African example deserves special attention in light of more than a thousand restricting laws.

South Africa is a country in a perpetual state of war. The majority of its people are without effective political power but possess a growing role in the economic and industrial life of the society. Consequently, the friction wrought by the irrepressible demands of freedom and the stubborn system of racial apartheid, has ignited South Africa from time to time. To protect its interests the government has slapped a series of biting legislative prohibitions on the black majority. Chimutengwende asserts correctly that these legislative shackles are meant to control what the media disseminate. However, he continues that the laws were not intended primarily for the media but rather to "protect and consolidate the system of apartheid and white rule as a whole" (Chimutengwende 1978, 57). We have followed Chimutengwende in enumerating the principal acts affecting the work of journalists.

bantu administration act (no. 38, 1927)

Under this act, the government may prevent any white journalist from collecting the news from any African living area. Numerous Western journalists have been ensnared by this broad legislative act. There have been at least four hundred proclamations "under which journalists have been arrested for writing on issues like political unrest, famine, and poor living

FIVE

conditions" (Chimutengwende 1978, 58).

The Bantu Administration Act allows the government to screen the journalists who write on the conditions of Africans. Although the journalists working in South Africa for Western media institutions have proved resourceful, they have frequently been forced to write only what the South African authorities allow them to write. Convincing the authorities that they are not going to criticize the South African system of racial apartheid becomes a major task for most journalists.

SUPPRESSION OF COMMUNISM ACT (NO 44, 1950)

The aim of this act had less to do with the economic theory of communism or the political dimensions of Marx, Engels or Lenin's doctrines than the suppression of popular protest by the African majority. In fact, the act "defined" communism as "any scheme which aimed to bring about any political, industrial, social or economic change with the union by promotion of disturbance or disorder, by unlawful acts of omission or by the threat of such acts or omissions or by means which include the promotion of disturbance or disorders, or such acts or omissions or threat." The act allows for the banning of individuals who are charged under the suppression of communism. Such a person cannot engage in journalism, popular writing of any kind and cannot be quoted. The government's decision to ban a journalist, shut down a newspaper or charge an individual with acts to promote the aims of communism is unappealable to any judicial authority.

PUBLIC SAFETY ACT (NO. 3, 1953)

The Public Safety Act of 1953, gave the government the right to declare a state of emergency without recourse to parliament. Anyone within the government's cabinet can ban individuals or organizations considered enemies of the apartheid system. Thus, arrests and detentions without trial are familiar instruments in the brutal hand of apartheid. Journalists and newspapers are regularly banned. The closing down of newspapers and the suppression of news considered likely to cause people to complain against the racist system are fixtures in the social and legal fabric of South Africa. It is a country whose legal texture is comprised of a series of public safety type laws that have little to do with the protection of the major public safety but rather the securing of privileges for the minority.

CRiMiNAl LAw AMENdMENT ACT (NO. 8, 1953)

Such is the audacity of the legal system in South Africa that the government makes it a crime for any person to advise, suggest, encourage or incite the public or an individual to protest against or campaign for the repeal of any of the legal restrictions placed on the masses of people. Consequently, there can be no newspaper articles, features or editorials which discuss the legal system which victimizes the black population. To avoid being banned or closed down, South African journalists impose self-censorship. When they refuse to back down as in the case of Allister Sparks, former editor of the *Rand Daily Mail* over the Muldergate information-peddling scandal, they lose their jobs by government pressure. Self-censorship is the predominant mode of editorial pressure on editors who live under the shadow of being closed down or banned. They censor themselves and therefore, the people are less knowledgeable than they would have been with a freer press.

CRiMiNAl pROCEdURE ANd EVidENCE ACT (NO. 56, 1955)

Under this act, journalists are forced to reveal the source of their information to any magistrate who requests it. If the journalist refuses, he or she may be jailed up to one year. Furthermore, if the journalist should appear and refuses to answer one question, the same imprisonment is possible. This law is designed to frighten journalists away from subjects which are embarrassing to the government. When a journalist knows that if he or she writes an article on the abuse of the prisoners at Robben Island or Walvis Bay he or she will be hauled before a magistrate and questioned, he or she is likely to think twice, maybe even thrice about writing such a story. So the public goes without any real investigative work on the prisons, the black townships, the guerilla war or industrial sabotage by black workers. There is a premium on ignorance which the South African government is willing to pay to maintain.

FIVE

RIOTOUS ASSEMBLIES ACT (NO. 17, 1956)
Any newspaper guilty of publishing or broadcasting any assembly which has been banned may be closed down. The Riotous Assemblies Act seeks to keep the public ignorant of any protest, planned or actual, which might show dissatisfaction with the apartheid regime. It is a crime to disseminate either whole or in part the speech or words of any person prohibited from attending public gatherings.

OFFICIAL SECRETS ACT (NO. 16, 1956) BOSS LAW (NO. 101, 1969)
According to these regulations, the Minister of Justice can declare any area or subject to be circumscribed. This means that no journalist or other person may take photographs or write stories about the area or subject. "Security matter" is the term most often used to circumscribe a subject. Thus, police matters, prisons, war activities or (BOSS) the Bureau for State Security, are off limits for public discussion.

POST OFFICE ACT (NO. 44, 1958, 1972, 1974)
BOSS is empowered through the Post Office to intercept and read postal articles, telegrams and news reports. In addition, all telephone messages are liable to be intercepted if BOSS believes the telephone messages are anti-government. Since 1949, the South African government has been intercepting telegrams and telephone messages it considers slanderous to the state (Chimutengwende 1978, 61).

PRISONS ACT (NO. 8, 1959)
No journalist is allowed to publish any article on the prisons of South Africa. It is a crime to photograph a prisoner, prisoners or a prison. This law was meant to stop all loop-holes not covered in the *Official Secrets Act*. Because of this law, there has rarely been an article detailing what is suspected of being one of the most heinous prison systems in the world. Such laws are generally made to prevent the revelation of unjustifiable practices.

EXTENSION OF UNIVERSITY EDUCATION ACT (NO. 45, 1959)

This act restricts the freedom of African students in communicating with their fellows. Black college students, unlike their counterparts are not permitted to publish, disseminate or otherwise broadcast their views without the express permission of the rector of the college. In effect, every magazine, newspaper, pamphlet or handout African students produce must be specifically approved by the rector. Furthermore, no statement regarding the students' conditions, complaints or problems can be issued without the rector's consent. *The Extension of University Act*, a title which belies its sinister character, actually is a restriction on the rights of students to freely associate and disseminate their views. A rector who grants students the permission to publish articles about the apartheid system may be convicted under a number of laws including the *Criminal Law Amendment Act* and the *Suppression of Communism Act*.

PUBLICATIONS AND ENTERTAINMENT ACT (NO. 26, 1963) AND THE PUBLICATIONS ACT (1974)

These two pieces of legislation were meant to knit together a legal pattern from which no person considered an enemy of the state could escape. Therefore, the *Publications and Entertainment Act of 1963* laid out the limits of undesirable publications. The definition included any material found to be indecent, obscene, offensive, harmful to public morals, blasphemous and offensive to the religious convictions of any section of the inhabitants of the Republic. Although the African population is approximately five times the size of the white population, the law was not meant to protect their moral or ethical sensibilities. The 1974 *Publication Act* furthered the restrictions on journalists and the public by extending the 1963 act to include films, photographs, records, stage shows and art works. The government is also empowered to restrict future issues of a publication which might be considered undesirable. There are regular tests of this law because of the inability of the courts to define precisely what is meant by "obscene," "offensive," "indecent" and "blasphemous." It almost goes without saying that the state sees these terms in line with Boer religious principles. Despite the use of the

FIVE

phrase "offensive to the religious convictions of any section of the inhabitants" in the law, the traditional or contemporary beliefs of Africans are not protected under this legislation.

CUSTOMS AND EXCISE ACT (NO. 91, 1964)
The *Customs and Excise Act* was created to deal with foreign publications, magazines, pamphlets and books. In order to bring foreign publishers in line with the policies of the government, the act makes it a crime to import foreign publications which are indecent or obscene or otherwise "objectionable" to the Publications Control Board. If materials are found crossing the borders, they may be confiscated and banned. By 1976, the Board had banned more than 20,000 publications since its inception in 1963. According to a report in the *Rand Daily Mail* (August 14, 1974) and the *Guardian* (August 23, 1976), the Publications Board had banned 638 out of 1208 publications submitted to it for scrutiny in 1973. Of such bannings in the history of the Publications Board, it was one of the lowest numbers.

DEFENSE AMENDMENT ACT (NO. 85, 1967)
Under this legislation no journalist can write about the military operations and activities of the South African army. During the South African occupation of Angola in 1981 and 1982, no reports could be printed in South African newspapers. Only through correspondents stationed in or accredited to Angola could the world read about South African involvement. Publication of anything which might cause the public to feel "threatened," "alarmed" or "depressed" is considered an offense to the government and is cause for prosecution. By 1982, the frequency of urban violence directed against the government had increased nearly four hundred percent over 1976, yet it was illegal for any writer to report such information. Because domestic reporters and foreign correspondents working in South Africa cannot report information which shows the government in a bad light, they often publish only government reports.

NEWSPAPER ANd IMPRINT REGISTRATION ACT (NO. 63, 1971)

The *Newspaper and Imprint Registration Act* is designed to head off at the gate publications which might disseminate materials which challenge apartheid. Therefore, before any newspaper can start operating, names and addresses of all former connections of the editors and personnel must be declared. In addition, the intended nature and contents of the publication must be expressed. Finally, a deposit of R10,000 to R20,000 is required if the Minister of Justice considers the newspaper a possible violator of the *Suppression of Communism Act*. No African newspaper has escaped this provision since its inception. According to Chimutengwende in May 1971, ten applicants for new newspapers were rejected because they could not afford the deposit demanded and subsequently had to cancel the launching of their publications (Chimutengwende 1978, 63). Since the deposit is not refundable, few black publishers can make a gift of R10,000 to R20,000 to the government to start publishing. Clearly, the act discourages journalists and publishers as it is intended to do in order to keep the whites from the stark realities of apartheid.

ACCESS RESTRAINTS

The South African government has many other ways to control access to the press. Because journalists, dependent upon government sanction to perform their work, do not like being out of work, they are less likely to report or reveal stories which are embarrassing to the government. Thus, self-censorship is a principal restraint on journalists working in South Africa.

At another level, the flow of information in South Africa is restricted by the Central News Agency, the dominant distributor of newspapers in South Africa. Its functions are to insure that foreign newspapers do not infringe upon South African law. Because foreign journalists do not write with South African laws in mind, this is a big job for the CNA selectors (deleters).

Alongside the CNA is the South African Press Association (SAPA); both organizations exist in a marginal marshland of journalistic soft walking. SAPA is a monopoly news agency and is owned by the Argus newspaper group. So both CNA and SAPA are monopolies which effectively control the press in

FIVE

South Africa as sort of a second line of defense from the ruling apartheid position.

Another way the South African government has restrained journalistic freedom is by arresting and banning editors and staff of newspapers. Journalists are harassed, abused and detained without trial. Consequently, a large white newspaper such as the *Rand Daily Mail* would hardly be closed because of the international outcry this would cause. Instead, their editors would be banned or arrested. As a point in fact, in June 1982, fifty white, foreign and local journalists were barred from Soweto. Yet smaller white newspapers and black newspapers are often closed because of their suspected anti-government positions.

THE AFRICAN PRESS

Black papers have existed in South Africa since 1884 when Jo Tengo Jabavu set up *Imvo Zabantsundu*. By 1904, John Dube had begun *Ilanga Law Natal*. Then in 1912, Walter Rabusana, a preacher, started *Izwi la Bantu*. Due to the unusual pressures under which South African blacks have lived, the newspapers have often been short-lived. They have encountered enormous hostility from the government.

In the sixties and seventies, *The World* captured international attention because of the resourcefulness and courage of Percy Qoboza who was forced to resign from his editorial post along with his entire staff because of opposition from the government to the views of *The World*. The paper was replaced by *The Post* which subsequently was replaced by *The Sowetan*. In effect, *The World*, *The Post* and *The Sowetan* are in the same tradition. The readership has remained constant as the paper has changed names, offices and editors. The unalterable direction of the press among black journalists is for liberation of the masses of the people through literacy, discussion, information and knowledge. This makes them constant targets of BOSS, the South African Security Agency. The aim of The Defense Act was to prevent journalists from reporting on any losses and set-backs suffered by the South African forces. Such reports, they believed, might cause public alarm.

Stan Motjuwadi, a journalist since 1956 and long-time editor of *Drum*

Magazine: South Africa, was detained without trial only once, a rarity for an editor who has worked that length of time. "I've been lucky," Motjuwadi told *The Herald*, April 16, 1982. But he was jailed, harassed, threatened, and beaten, like most black journalists in South Africa. Until 1988 at any one time, there were 100,000 people in jail for violating apartheid's laws. Motjuwadi, echoing others said, "There is no freedom of the press. We can't do our jobs properly because there is this mass of laws" (*Herald*, April 6, 1982). Motjuwadi is just one of a strong cadre of intelligent and dynamic black journalists that has been victimized by the South African laws.

THE STEYN COMMISSION

South Africa is pre-eminently a society of laws. The government exercises totalitarian control over the lives of the people, even legislating on every aspect of the press and thereby restricting the right of the people to information. In 1981, the government appointed a mass media committee to investigate ways of restraining the press inasmuch as the reporting of Namibian military maneuvers and Angolan invasions by the South African army had caused a worldwide reaction. In early 1982, the Steyn Commission, as it was called, recommended the compulsory registration of journalists with a government register and the creation of a tribunal which would discipline journalists (*The Herald*, February 3, 1982). One of the first reactions against the Steyn Commission came from the Black Media Workers' Association (MWASA). The acting president, Goba Ndhlovu, rejected the commission's report and recommendations outright, saying that the findings were an attempt to justify actions taken against MWASA in the past and actions they planned to take in the future. Ndhlovu further stated that it was his belief "that there can never be justice in an unjust society" (*The Herald*, February 3, 1982). Following MWASA's strong condemnation a group of white editors also rejected the Steyn Commission's call for a statutory press council and a government register of journalists. Seventeen editors of the largest papers in South Africa signed a statement of rejection to no avail.

Nearly 60% of all white South Africans work in one capacity or another to maintain one of the most bureaucratic societies in the world. There are

FIVE

numerous boards, agencies and commissions to regulate and to monitor the Draconian network of interlocking laws to control the people and the press. The Steyn Commission was appointed in recognition by the government of the ever growing influence of the press even with controls. The black press has been particularly fearless in its portrayal of the conditions under which Africans live in the society. In addition to the long list of African reporters and editors who have been harassed, banned, jailed, and beaten, there are some white editors who have suffered similar fates. A few, like Donald Woods, editor of the *East London Daily Dispatch*, although banned until October 31, 1982, have managed to protest the lack of press freedom while living in exile.

Woods had written an article "Biko, the greatest man I have ever known," which was reprinted in the *Cape Times*, September 9, 1977 in which he said, "I once went to Mr. J. T. Kruger and begged him to lift the restrictions on Steven and to speak to him. The result of that visit was an increase in Steve's restrictions and a state prosecution against me" (*Cape Times*, September 9, 1977).

The South African government is relentless in its attacks on the press. It closed down *The World*, the largest black newspaper in South Africa, as well as its companion paper, the *Weekend World*, and detained its editor, Percy Qoboza. This intensification of government interference in the press during the late 1970s and into the 80s was a direct result of the clashing political and social turmoil in the country. Allistar Sparks, former editor of the *Rand Daily Mail*, once vowed to keep on fighting the struggle against press harassment until the government changed its course (Pollak 1980, 96). A few months later Sparks was forced out of his editorship and was hired as a correspondent for the *Washington Post*. In 1990, perhaps as a sign of times to come, Sparks announced that he would visit South Africa.

The Steyn Commission notwithstanding the campaign for a free press in South Africa will be intensified. Support of the government's bannings and banishings of editors who disagree with government policy makes the Steyn Commission an added instrument for the propagation of a negative view of the press in South Africa. As such, it fuels the fires for press freedom.

six

PROBLEMS AND PREROGATIVES

THE MASS media in Africa are not without problems, both created and inherited. Yet the contributions to be made to development on the continent by the media are enormous. Hachten and Legum have documented the oppressive manner in which the colonial powers controlled the press, providing an unfortunate legacy which is difficult to remove. Indeed, Hachten says that the newspapers "were subjected to harsh and often arbitrary controls by colonial officials" (Hachten 1970, 25). Legum explains "all the colonial governments, without exception, maintained severe forms of censorship, either directly, as in Francophone countries, or indirectly through sedition and other laws" (Legum 1971, 29). The colonial powers understood the value of the press to the free wills of the masses and feared the unbridled use of the media by Africans.

The press has historically been a key component in political ascendancy. It was used by Lenin who developed his influence by controlling *Iskra* prior to 1917; Hitler used the press magnate Hugenberg to help advance his career, and Mussolini was editor of *Avanti*. In the United States, numerous politicians have used the press to their advantage. There is no question that Azikiwe of Nigeria, editor of *West African Pilot* and Blaise Diagne of Senegal

SIX

who had his own paper, were following a tried path. Many African leaders rose to power on the printed word. The press constitutes an important leverage for attaining, consolidating and maintaining power. Because of its unique position in the constituency of political power, most politicians want to control the press. In their quest to control, they often abuse reporters, limit press access and harass reporters who seek to serve their government, their people and their consciences.

problems of the media

Peter Enahoro, editor of *Africa Now*, quit the Lagos *Daily Times* after a conflict with the early military authorities. The military finally took the major shares of the newspaper despite its prestige as one of the best newspapers in Africa. Enahoro, perhaps, in the top echelons of African journalists, was a loss to the Nigerian scene. During the time that Alhaji Babatunde Jose was chairman of the Board at *Daily Times*; with Dele Cole as editor and Dr. Doyin Aboaba features editor, the newspaper ranked among the best in the world and was probably the top newspaper at the time in Africa. Alhaji Jose said of the military regime's pressure that the press was operating under considerable restraints even though it was still the freest in Africa. The vagaries of government harassment have occurred throughout Africa.

The *Legon Observer* in Ghana noted in 1974, in its opinion, that during the preceding twelve months it had experienced all kinds of interference, sometimes direct, sometimes indirect; official and unofficial; subtle as well as crude. In Uganda, an editor was handcuffed to a steering wheel and strangled for articles in his paper. The Ethiopian government fined an editor for putting the photo of a minister on the same page with a prize bull. According to the law of Malawi, a person can get life imprisonment for sending "false information" outside of the country.

In Egypt, *Al Akhbar* published by Mustafa and Ali Amin has been under attack during several governments. In 1950, Mustafa was arrested 21 times. In 1960, President Nasser nationalized his publishing company. In 1965, Nasser charged him with 165 crimes. President Sadat freed him in 1974. Mustafa was quoted in the *International Herald Tribune*, April 8, 1982:

PROBLEMS AND PREROGATIVES

A free press is a light in the darkness. As far as democracy goes, America had it when its illiteracy rate was as high as Egypt's. If we wait until every Egyptian has a Ph.D. we'll never have democracy.

The Kenyan Press, once regarded as relatively unrestricted, has come under increasing pressure in the last few years. After the death of President Jomo Kenyatta, widely hailed, though often disputed, as the leader of Kenya's drive for independence, Daniel Arap Moi was elected by the Parliament to succeed him.

Moi's relationship with the Kenyan press has been turbulent to say the least. Although nominally a democratic capitalist country, Kenya has emerged as one of the most aggressive governments against journalists and intellectuals. Moi's attempt to consolidate his political power after the death of the nation's first president meant the suppression of numerous journalists, students and academics.

Beginning in the spring of 1982, Kenyan authorities swooped down on unsuspecting university lecturers and arrested them for teaching "seditious" material. Most of the arrested academics had their homes searched for books considered anti-Kenyan and their offices were ransacked for their reading lists. Attacks on the university academics have occurred periodically in Kenya's recent history. As in many other African nations, the university has been closed several times by oppressive regimes.

The arrest of Ngugi Wa Thiong'o, one of Africa's most celebrated writers, by Jomo Kenyatta stunned the intellectual community. But, it was only a prelude to a more exacting suppression of intellectual freedom to come during the reign of President Moi. Coincidentally, many of Moi's most repressive acts occurred while he was serving as the chairman of the Organization of African Unity.

Throughout his tenure, veiled threats against opposing political and intellectual leaders occurred until he eventually outlawed all political parties other than Kanu, his own, forcing veteran politicians like Oginga Odinga to attack the policy as a policy of fear. Subsequently, Moi declared Kenya a one-party state and began a campaign to silence his critics. Six popular

SIX

university lecturers, including Al-Amin Mazrui, the nephew of political scientist Ali Mazrui, were detained without trial. Other intellectuals such as Michere Mugo and Ngugi Wa Thiong'o fled into exile. Maina wa Kinyatti was imprisoned until 1989.

The editor of the *Nairobi Standard*, George Githii, was dismissed in line with what has become under Moi an editorial hot seat. Hilary Ngweno, a well-known producer and journalist, has been effectively silenced and the authors Ngugi Wa Thiong'o and Michere Mugo have been barred from having their plays performed. Such are the realities of the press and pen in Kenya.

An attempted *coup d'etat* in early August, 1982 was probably more a sign of the deep discontent the people felt over the erosion of their freedoms than any ideological movement. The ideology as expressed in the streets of Nairobi's poorer sections was simply "power!" There had been an attempted coup by air force officers.

Moi's response was quick and heavy handed. Instead of finding a lesson in the rebellion, he imposed stiffer repressive measures which cowed the civilian population and then proceeded to arrest the entire 2,100-member air force. It is still too early to tell what the lasting effect of these measures will be for the nation. What is certain, however, is that Kenya can no longer be thought of, if ever it was, as a nation with press and intellectual freedom of the sort that tolerates political criticism of the government.

Vincent Mijoni, editor of *Daily Mail* in Lusaka, was brought before parliament in 1976 to explain why he had headlined a story "MP's boob!" He answered that democracy is "a two-way traffic between leaders and the people and that freedom of expression has many tongues, the strongest of which is truth." Six years later in Lusaka, Naphy Nyalugwe, editor of *The Times of Zambia*, was arrested for publishing false information. He published a story that a truckload of weapons had been stolen from military barracks on June 22, 1981. He was arrested in February 1982 (*The Herald*, February 20, 1982).

Thami Mazwai, news editor of *The Sowetan*, was jailed for 18 months for refusing to testify at a terror trial (*The Herald*, February 20, 1982). In addition, South Africa arrested Nathan Clifford Gibson, bureau chief of United Press Internation (UPI) because of contraventions of The Defense Act. He was accused of wrongfully publishing a statement related to activities of The South African Defense Force (*The Herald*, February 20, 1982).

Of the nearly two hundred and fifty newspapers in Africa, a mere fraction of the nearly two thousand in the United States, clearly half of them have experienced interference by the government. To some extent, this may be attributed to the lack of journalism training, which may cause conflict with governments because of poor knowledge of laws and regulations. A Zimbabwean journalist trained in the United States will have a different response to some issues than one trained in Zimbabwe. In Zimbabwe a journalist may not publish statements attributed to "sources" or "informed sources." Sources must always be named.

The problem of intimidation and harassment of media specialists is a growing one throughout Africa as it is in the rest of the world. But in Africa, besides this general problem of media personnel, there are some fundamental problems which should be examined.

NEWSPRINT

Nearly 90% of all newsprint used in Africa is imported. The bulk of the imported newsprint comes from the Scandinavian countries, among the major exporters of newsprint. In 1974, the Scandinavian nations reduced their total export allocation to the whole of Africa from 62,000 tons to 19,600 tons. To prevent large African users like Egypt from overbuying and re-exporting, the Scandinavian countries reduced their amount to the entire continent. Even with 100,000 tons to the continent, Africa would be newsprint poor compared to the United States which used ten million tons per year. Of course, until literacy increases and the productive capacities of the nations are enlarged, Africa's share of the newsprint allocation might as well remain low.

SIX

multi-linguality

The overwhelming number of indigenous languages makes broadcasting electronically or through print an extremely trying enterprise. In Zaire alone, there are up to 500 languages (Metrowich 1975, 340). Nigeria has another 250 languages. With such wide diversity of languages, although there are a few lingua francas, many people will rarely read a newspaper, listen to a radio or watch a television in their first language. Many of these people will never know that newspapers could be published in their language. Some languages still do not have written alphabets. Thus, one of the serious problems facing the media communicationist in Africa is the language problem. Most newspapers that reach a wide audience are in English, French, Portuguese, or Arabic, none of which is indigenous to Africa. Furthermore, high illiteracy makes dependency on newspapers for information less reliable for development than radio and television.

high production costs

In 1973, Barton estimated that from 1963 to 1973 the number of African newspapers had declined from 240 to 107. Although Barton, typically supportive of British colonial policy, said that the decline existed because of political pressure. That was not the major reason. A few papers had been forced to close their doors because of confrontation with the government but most were forced to shut down because of the high cost of production. Rising energy prices, rising newsprint costs, and domestic wage inflation have been the principle contributors to production costs. Since most African nations import print and electronic broadcasting equipment from thousands of miles away, unlike the industrialized countries, they must pay the added expense of not producing their own equipment. Tanzania has long said that television was an expensive luxury. On the other hand, oil-rich Gabon has television but no daily newspaper.

Lack of local material for television

The great seducer for most media-wise Africans is the television. It operates as an open system gobbling up local and foreign talent each minute it is on the air. The problem inherent in this is the invitation to foreign propaganda and information. Without local skill, the television must look to the industrialized and media sophisticated nations for programming. Radio programmers in major African capitals receive taped materials in abundance through the national transcription services of BBC, Voice of America, British Central Office of Information, Canadian Broadcasting Corporation, Radio Peking, and Radio Moscow. VOA does 72 hours a week for foreign distribution. Television programmers in Africa receive catalogs of film less expensive than in America or Europe. In addition, newsreels are often freely distributed.

Prospects

The characteristics of media systems depend on a wide range of conditions: (1) The cultural factor, (2) the political factor, and (3) the economic factor. Most African nations possess a multiplicity of cultures within their borders, the legacy of the European state systems imposed during the colonial period. These cultures are often historically, though not necessarily contemporarily, antagonistic, as for example, the Shona and Ndebele of Zimbabwe; the Ga and Asante of Ghana, the Tutsi and the Hutu of Burundi-Rwanda. In the majority of cases, the antagonisms date back more than a century. However, there are instances of modern religious and cultural conflict such as the Hausa-Ibo confrontations of the 1960's in Nigeria.

A media system must be able to accommodate the inherent cultural contradictions in the modern African state if it is to satisfy the demands of the people. Otherwise, the system creates rather than eradicates cultural divisions. Recognition of cultural diversity is the first principle in establishing a representative media. Not to recognize difference is to impose the culture of the ruling majority on the minorities.

There are several ways a nation might choose to deal with the factor of cultural diversity. Nigeria, for example, has a daily newspaper for most of the states in the federal unions. In addition, some of the major newspaper organizations such as the *National Concord* group publishes in several of the vernacular languages. Tanzania's most popular paper is printed in Kiswahili, the language of the majority of the people. In this way, the regional cultural distinctions are minimized and the unity of the nation is encouraged through use of a national language. However, in countries such as Cameroons and Zaire, there is no one language spoken by 90% or more of the people as in Tanzania and consequently in those nations the press uses French, the colonial language. Actually, in the Cameroons, French or English may be used as Bamun and Bamileke and other languages would only serve to emphasize cultural difference. It is an ironic fact that the colonial languages have served the purpose of national cohesion in most cases.

The political factor refers to the traditional as well as contemporary political culture of a nation. Malawi, a landlocked, mountainous country in East Africa, is the personal fiefdom of President-for-life Kamuzu Banda. The press owes its allegiance directly to Banda. He succeeded in having the Malawian parliamentarians, all subject to him, pass a law imprisoning a person for life if such a person was found publishing a false report. President Banda was granted the right to be the arbiter of truth or falsehood (Wilcox 1975, 90). In nations where the ruler or ruling party determines truth or falsehood, the consequences of presenting an alternative view can be dangerous. Journalists are human, however, and despite their best efforts to present fair assessments of conditions within a nation frequently allow their prejudices to slip into the reporting. If a certain ruler is particularly arbitrary in his behavior toward the people, journalists might find him to be an extra good subject for their own moral sentiment. A journalist with racialist feelings might report Zimbabwe's multi-racial efforts negatively and South Africa's apartheid favorably. These are the dangers of imbalanced judgments. The ruler who is cruel should be reported as fairly as the one who is kind. A capitalist and a communist must be given equally fair treatment in a respectable press. This does not mean that journalists do not have an opinion, most journalists are extremely opinionated. It means that the journalist tries to hold personal opinions in abeyance when writing a story.

In this way, personal political views are not presented as journalism. Working journalists are not rhetoricians, using their own ethical standards and judgments to assess the information presented. They are intelligent, broadminded intellectuals who present the facts in a way that the audience has all the information needed to make an informed judgment.

The economic factor comprises the financial and material conditions of a nation. Without facilities and financial backing a media system is limited in its ability to deliver services to all of a nation's people. Thus, the economic factor is the blood of all media systems whether state-controlled or privately controlled. The reasons for this are fairly obvious. Journalists must be fed regardless of the political or cultural traditions of a nation. It is easy to see that the more money a media system has from the public or private sector the more effective it could be in the transmission of information to the nation. Indeed, in some nations, daily newspapers are not feasible for financial reasons. The question of expensive electronic media is often controlled by the amount of money a government is willing to divert from high priority developmental projects in other sectors.

Media obstacles in Africa are probably more numerous and fundamental than on any other continent. Almost every African state has technical or financial obstacles in the media professions. Avoiding the hurdles becomes impossible without the necessary financial and political freedom needed to maintain viable organizations. Therefore, most media systems are tripped up by enormous hurdles, some of which, if not successfully dealt with in Europe and North America, are under control in those continents.

The DNA of any media system is its domestic and international communication infrastructure, inasmuch as the ability to gather information quickly and to disseminate it just as quickly is basic to the communication process. Whenever a system is unable to deliver, it is next to useless.

Poor communications within African countries and between countries represent a major obstacle. It is still easier to communicate between Kinshasa and Brussels than it is to communicate between Kinshasa and Bujumbura. Furthermore, Kinshasa has no direct links to Nairobi, Nairobi no direct links to Yaounde. But there are direct links from Kinshasa, Nairobi, Luanda, and

Abidjan to Brussels, London, Lisbon, and Paris. The situation described above is not atypical throughout the continent, it remains the norm that African capitals are tied to European capitals and not to each other by virtue of the colonial legacy.

Internally, most communication systems lack the necessary infrastructure for gathering or distributing news to the nation. One can get the *London Times* in Harare quicker than a Zimbabwean living in Chipinga can receive *The Herald*, though fortunately for Zimbabwe, because of the road and transport system, not too much quicker. In other countries the situation is bleak indeed. Some areas of countries like Angola, Zaire, Mozambique, which are hundreds of miles from the administrative centers do not know that newspapers exist. College students in Dakar may be reading the Paris *Le Monde* but in the south of Senegal the people live their lives without once knowing or caring that Dakar has a daily newspaper.

External communications are poor because the telecommunications systems are not yet well developed. Furthermore, of the twenty-eight landlocked nations in the world, fourteen of them are African states. It will take considerable effort and vision on the part of African states to overcome the problems of inaccessibility, whether it is caused by lack of an infrastructure or being landlocked. Several states have now introduced satellite systems which have greatly improved international communications. But satellite systems are expensive and few African nations can afford to operate them. Nevertheless, the oil-rich nations such as Nigeria, Algeria, Egypt, and Libya have invested in improved communication systems. On the other hand, one of the poorest nations in Africa, *Tanzania* started the Mwenge Earth Satellite station in 1979.

It is obvious that geographical inaccessibility impedes the gathering and distribution of news. Some areas of Angola, for example, require up to three weeks for mail to arrive from Luanda. The pattern is repeated throughout Africa. Many places remain totally inaccessible to modern print news although radio had made powerful inroads. Urban media professionals often disregard the rural areas. Yet journalists and journalism trainers such as Alfred Opubor, Ezekiel Makunike, and Paul Ansah contend that the information gathered from the rural districts aids in solidifying the national image by fusing solidarity between the rural areas and the urban areas. News reaching the rural areas from the urban centers establishes the cultural and political presence of the government.

Once a newspaper is printed, the publisher must decide how to deliver it to the readers. The most common delivery system in Africa is road transportation. This means that a newspaper published in Lagos, Nigeria, which came off the presses at twelve o'clock midnight would arrive in Sokoto in the north of the country by 10 o'clock at night! National delivery however is not an issue in most African countries. In some nations, there are several dailies operating in major towns. For example, in Zimbabwe, daily newspapers operate in Umtali, Bulawayo and Harare. There is no demand for the *Herald* published in Harare to be distributed in Bulawayo or for the *Chronicle* in Bulawayo to be distributed in Salisbury. There does not exist a national newspaper and consequently no demand for long distance deliveries.

The *Herald* prints 100,000 copies a day and has nearly a million readers, all of them within a twenty-mile radius of downtown Salisbury. Other nations have several dailies operating in different regions of the country and a few of them aspire to national coverage. In Nigeria, *The National Concord* and the *Daily Times* are two examples. Still other nations have a party paper which operates as the national paper. However, only where there is some demand for the paper nationally is the problem of transportation likely to be severe. A relatively wealthy private newspaper like *The National Concord* in Nigeria can afford to distribute its copies throughout the country by airplane dispatch.

The lack of trained journalists represents another major obstacle in African media. Only since the early 1970's has there been a concerted effort to train journalists. Sparked initially by UNESCO and the International Press Institute's workshops for journalists, several nations established their own institutes for training journalists. The most impressive of these remains the Kenyan Institute for Mass Communication.

SEVEN

THE POTENTIAL FOR PRESS FREEDOM

politics and media

FRANK BARTON'S assessment that "there is no press freedom in Black Africa in any recognizable form" is certainly an erroneous overstatement (Metrowich 1975, 340). If Barton had meant "Western form," he would have also been incorrect since the press in Liberia, Ghana, Nigeria and Kenya in 1975 when he made the statement enjoyed press freedoms of the sort he would consider Western. Of course, if he were thinking of the negative attitudes of political leaders towards the press, then he could have found the same antipathy among European and American leaders.

Media institutions are products of the political systems which create them. Any meaningful discussion of the media systems cannot be addressed without reference to the political ideology. As Aboaba has contended, "in this contest, the emphasis is on the characteristics and ideology of the political system involved, not on the characteristics of the media system" (Aboaba 1979, 8).

THE POTENTIAL FOR PRESS FREEDOM

One of the earliest American media theorists argued for rigid classification of media systems. Thus, Schramm could draw a clear distinction between American and Soviet views of the media in the 1950's.

> We are apt to think that people must and should hold different ideas and values and therefore to encourage the arts of compromise and majority rule; the Soviet Russians are apt to think that men should hold different viewpoints, that compromise is a sign of weakness, that there is one right position to be found in Marxist interpretation and to be depended, propagated and enforced (Schramm 1956, 107).

This became the dominant cold war view of reality. As we have come to know, the world is not so neatly divided among American and Soviet ideologies; there are other viewpoints, other ideas and attitudes. While some writers have spoken of authoritarian, totalitarian, social responsibility, libertarian and evolving perspectives of the media, we prefer to believe that media are either (1) *unrestrained*, (2) *restrained* or (3) *directed* (see Appendix C). By *unrestrained*, we mean that the media operate according to their own values, norms and objectives. A *restrained* media is controlled by the government. To be *directed* means that the media operate under the influence of the government's stated objectives for national development. The latter perspective is found throughout Africa.

In a recent book, Black and Whitney (1988) have discussed press theories as revolutionary, developmental and democratic socialist. What they mean by revolutionary is that the press "is managed by people who feel alienated from the government" and "is not necessarily authoritarian or libertarian in nature" (p. 536). The developmental press "reflects modern nationalist and political independence movements, and draws upon socialist thought and developmental principle" (p. 536). According to Black and Whitney, the democratic socialist theory is a modified form of what has been called the social responsibility theory. The aim of this theory is to accommodate the media systems in Scandinavia and other socialist regions of Europe which do not conform to the social responsibility theory (p. 536).

SEVEN

We have essentially rejected these Eurocentric formulations in our discussion of African media because they grossly skew the nature of media institutions to the European example. For instance, no African nation is conceivably within the social responsibility model which is considered the "best" example of a responsible media. However, from an African viewpoint, the media in a few nations would deny their social responsibility.

Therefore, we have used the concepts of *unrestrained, restrained,* or *directed* to provide an essentially value-free classification.

Africa is a complex and complicated continent in terms of media philosophies and management. Certainly there are numerous abuses of the press in various nations. Indeed, there are those who would contend that media which do not submit to the government's direction be severely punished. In fact, there are instances where such media have been banned. Lord Roy Thompson states convincingly that:

> in some of the new nations of the world, criticism of government may legitimately be subject to some degree of restriction. Some of the journalists in these developing countries do not have sufficient background of knowledge, experience and judgment to enable them to restrain themselves from destructive or inflammatory criticism which, exposed to populations which have not yet learned the art of political stability, could lead to serious unrest and even revolutionary activity (Sommerlad 1966, 143).

This perspective is supported by Lucien Pye who argued that oppositional media is usually unconstructive and hostile to government (Pye 1963).

The question of press freedom was pointedly taken up prior to the approval in 1980 of the new Nigeria constitution. According to Aboaba (1979):

> In a memorandum to the constituent Assembly, Mr. Felix Adenaike, general manager of the state-government owned *Sketch* group of publications and Mr. Femi Ogunsanwo, a political correspondent of

the *Daily Times* emphasized that what they were concerned with is not "absolute freedom to publish," which no constitution could allow, but protection for newspapers against apparently constitutional, but restrictive legislation by "temporary majorities."

In the end, the Constituent Assembly, in its final draft of the Nigerian constitution, excluded any special guarantee of press freedom. The Assembly wrote that "while the majority of the members felt the need to protect the freedom of the press, they did not feel that there were grounds for giving any Nigerian citizen a lesser right to freedom of expression than any other citizen who happens to be a newspaper editor or reporter. . . ." (Report of the Constitution Assembly Committee, Vol. 1, 1976, p. xvi).

Doyin Aboaba has contended that there are a few universally objective standards by which any press system can be judged (Aboaba, 1979). She investigated the basic question of the extent to which
military governments in Nigeria stifled press freedom. Were Nigerian journalists able to criticize inefficiency in government, and to stimulate public opinion under the military regime? Such questions could be asked about the overwhelming majority of African governments since more than thirty of them have or have had military administrations. In Nigeria, the role of the press has varied greatly depending upon the political climate surrounding military take-overs. Since Nigeria has had both military and civilian governments, it was an excellent laboratory for Aboaba's study of the African press.

She found that under the military government of General Aguiyi Ironsi, the first military leader to assume political power over the nation, the press aided in rebuilding a fragmented country. In her view, the press did not become overly critical of the government because the political climate was one of collective constructive growth. Everyone had anticipated a *coup d'etat*, so Ironsi initially enjoyed a political honeymoon. The press afforded him the opportunity to consolidate, if he could, his position and to calm the fears of the country.

There had been quite remarkable precedents for the press seeking to advance the collective national goals of Africans. In reality, however, the press had only done so in connection with national movements for independence. *The Accra Evening News* in Ghana was the organ of Kwame Nkrumah's Convention People's Party and the *West African Pilot* in Nigeria played the same role for Nnamdi Azikiwe is National Conference for Nigeria and Cameroon. Kenya's Jomo Kenyatta used the pages of *Nuigwthania* for agitation against the colonists. Numerous other examples can be mentioned. Aboaba thinks that "in times of national crisis like the demise of civilian rule in Nigeria" the press responds as it is expected to respond: in defense of the collective good (Aboaba 1979, 98).

press freedom

The term "press freedom" refers to a journalist's *capacity*, *opportunity* and *willingness* to express her or his views without intimidation. Aboaba calls such freedom "adversary criticism of the government" which is made possible by the journalist's ability (Aboaba 1979).

press control

Press control may comprise three types of restraints: (1) legislative acts, (2) censorship, or (3) self-censorship. Certain laws of sedition and libel may be used to gag the press rather than protect individual rights. In addition, overt censorship may occur when certain stories are removed from the media. On the other hand, self-censorship is a result of fear of detention or bodily harm. In Africa, self-censorship appears to be the most common form of restraint. If one takes the South African case as an example, it is clear that (out of the 24 major papers) the newspapers that remain in business are the ones that have learned how to censor themselves. But, South Africa is not alone in this type of self-censorship. Newspapers in Malawi, Kenya, and Ivory Coast, among other nations, must exercise caution.

THE NIGERIAN CASE

Although the cultural heritage of the press may have come from the traditional courts of ancient kingdoms where the news carrier, messenger, and drummer were part of the King's entourage, acting on his behalf and for his benefit, the press laws of the country were initially derived from British Common Law (Aboaba 1979). Even after independence in 1960, Nigeria did not have constitutional protection for press freedom. There was in the 1963 Constitution a paraphrase of the Universal Declaration of Human Rights Article 19 which said:

> Every person shall be entitled to freedom of expression, including freedom to hold opinions and to receive and impart ideas and information without interference. (Section 25 (1) 1963 Nigerian Constitution)

Inasmuch as the initial perspective on press freedom in Nigeria came from the British Common Law, it would be valuable to examine British Common Law on this issue. J. Holland (1978) wrote that press freedom under the new law meant "freedom to print without previous license and freedom from undue legal restraint." The press had no special rights under this law; what was applicable to the citizenry in general was applicable to the press. Nigeria has kept this basic pattern for its press.

A person wishing to start a newspaper, for example, is under no press censorship or prior constraints on publication. Nevertheless, the publisher must swear an affidavit before a judicial officer declaring his name, the name of the newspaper, a description of the newspaper's facilities and make a deposit of 500 Naira or otherwise execute a bond equivalent to that amount, in order to begin publishing. The bond serves as a guarantee of any penalty or damages which may be assessed against the publisher in connection with the publication of the paper.

Providing the paper violates no rules or laws such as those prohibiting defamation, libel or sedition, the paper is free to publish whatever it wishes.

SEVEN

But as Aboaba (1979) points out, these provisions "do not always work out fairly in practice."

The Nigerian Press has not been without its legal difficulties. A number of restrictions have been placed on the press in Nigeria. The Official Secret Act of 1962 and The Newspaper (Amendment) Act of 1964 technically constituted formidable legal restraints. The Official Secret Act forbade the obtaining, retention, reproduction or transmission without lawful authority of any matter classified as secret by the government. Violation of this law carried fourteen years of imprisonment.

At issue is what is considered secret, classified or prejudicial to the government. Since any officer of the government might declare information to be prejudicial without an objective base, a publisher could be placed in jeopardy at will. The fact is that the government of the moment could influence the execution of legal matters out of self interest.

As serious as the Official Secret Act of 1962 was for the press, the 1964 Newspapers (Amendment) Act meant much more trouble. The portion of the act which creates controversy reads as follows:

> (1) Any person who authorizes for publication, publishes, reproduces or circulates for sale in a newspaper any statement, rumor or report knowing or having reason to believe that such statement, rumor or report is false shall be guilty of an offense and liable on conviction to a fine of 400 Naira or to imprisonment for a term of one year . . .
> (2) It shall be no defense to a charge under this section that he did not know or did not have reason to believe that the statement, rumor or report was false unless he proves that prior to publication, he took reasonable measures to verify the accuracy of such statement, rumor or report . . . (Elias 1969).

This law creates undue pressure for editors who must check the accuracy of their reporters' articles. The nature of the newspaper business with its editing, copy editing and time constraints makes it highly unlikely that any editor would devote "reasonable measures" to fore-checking every article.

The effect of the law is self-censorship; editors and publishers refuse to publish if they think they will be prosecuted. Press freedom is consequently impeded as much as it would be if government censorship were imposed. The conviction of Dr. Chike Obi for sedition, the legal battles of Mr. Amakiri from Bendel and the detention of Dr. Tai Solarin, to name a few celebrated cases, reflect the unsettled nature of Nigeria's relationship to the press. With the adoption in 1980 of the new Federal Constitution, it became more difficult for the executive to disregard the legal rights of any citizen, even journalists, for political reasons. Since the new constitution has been in effect, there has not been the type of wholesale attacks on the press as prior to 1980 although numerous politicians have criticized the press in no uncertain terms. The *National Concord*, edited at the time by Dr. Doyin Aboaba Abiola, came under severe attack in 1981 for a lengthy critique of the political life of Chief Obafemi Awolowo.

Overall, the Nigerian Press, even with the legacy of the British Common Law and several restricting pieces of legislation in its past, has been active, combative, and capable. Under the disposed civilian leader, President Shagari, the press flourished, protected in part by the right to trial. Since President Shagari, Nigeria has had governments by two military leaders, General Buhari and General Babangida. Both have been wary of the press.

zimbabwe: desettlerizing the media

The majority government of Zimbabwe inherited a well-established media network at independence in April, 1980. But, the task confronting the newly elected popular government was different from the prevailing problems of the media in African nations. What Zimbabwe faced was an entrenched elitist and urban media network meant to serve the minority white population and to serve as a connecting link between farmers. Thus, access to the existing media was almost exclusively the right of the white minority with television being limited and newspapers limited to the urban English speaking population.

During the period of the Unilateral Declaration of Independence of

SEVEN

Rhodesia (UDI), Ian Smith's regime used the media as a weapon of political, ideological and psychological warfare in an effort to maintain the regime in power. However, since Africans owned few television sets and rarely read the white newspapers, the Rhodesian propaganda had little effect on the independence struggle.

Nevertheless, Prime Minister Mugabe's government received operable TV and radio networks, modern movie theaters, several fully functioning newspapers, and an efficient communication infrastructure. These developments, however, were largely limited to the urban areas, where only 20% of the total population of nearly nine million lived. In addition, the media were in the hands of whites who owned, controlled or directed them. Ezekiel Makunike, the former director of the Zimbabwe Institute of Mass Communication put it sharply, "Under Smith, our voice was silenced" (Asante, et. al. 1982, 11). As a result, the media facilities were excellent but the media personnel and policies had to be desettlerized. Furthermore, the government had to develop a mechanism for desettlerizing the media without assuming direct control of the media itself.

THE MEDIA TRUST

A media trust functions independently of government and is comprised of individuals who have no personal financial stake in the media. Its obligation is to provide the people of the nation with a free, independent and responsible voice.

The Zimbabwe Mass Media Trust is undoubtedly a unique institution within the wide varieties of media structures and management systems. In 1980, when the popular government came to power, the most important daily and Sunday papers were published by the Rhodesian Printing Company, which became Zimbabwe Newspapers Ltd. on May 30, 1980. The major shareholder in the company was the South African Argus group.

The new government had to decide how to organize the desettlerization of the media and effect a transition of control over the newspapers in order to have them serve the purpose of national development. The same objective was envisioned for the Inter-Africa News Agency (Private) whose main contract for all outside news was with the South African Press Association (SAPA). Among the options facing the government was the creation of an autonomous body which, outside of direct government supervision, would exercise control of the media in Zimbabwe, both in terms of commercial operation and of editorial guidance. The government accepted this option and its acceptance led to the establishment of the Mass Media Trust. Subsequently, the Trust received funds from the government with which to purchase the Argus group shareholding in Zimbabwe Newspapers Ltd., together with the shares of other South African interests.

Simultaneously with the purchasing of the Argus shares, the Mass Media Trust became the supervising unit for the newly created Zimbabwe Inter-Africa News Agency (ZIANA) and the Zimbabwe Institute of Mass Communication, the training arm of the entire communication enterprise.

The Trust had five significant objectives:

1. Purchase all issued shares in ZIANA.
2. Purchase the shareholdings in Zimbabwe Newspapers Ltd.
3. Exercise all rights as shareholder of the said companies.
4. Form, organize and control the Institute of Mass Communication for the Training of Mass Media Personnel.
5. Carry out all activity similar or related to the foregoing or any activity deemed by the Trustees to be conducive to furthering the media welfare of the people of Zimbabwe, including acquisitions control, or participation in other organizations, associations or bodies.

The Board of Trustees is composed of seven members, appointed in an honorary capacity. The Trust's constitution prohibits any Trustee from being a member of parliament, a member of public services, or of the uniformed services. An Executive Secretary with a staff of five administrative assistants runs the daily operations of the Trust. Initially, the government named the Chair of the Trust, the Executive Secretary and one member of the board, who themselves named the other members of the Trust. The Trust's constitution empowers the Trustees to name their future chairperson. Dr.

SEVEN

Davison Sadza, a prominent medical doctor, was appointed chairman of the Trust. Mr. Akim Marere, a lawyer, was the first executive secretary of the Trust.

As the main shareholder of Zimbabwe Newspapers Ltd. with an initial 45.7 percent of the shares, the Trust effectively controls the company. This means that the Trust has the right to appoint editors and directors of the company's papers, and to define the policy guidelines for the paper. The Trust controls two dailies with a circulation of 140,000, two Sunday papers with a circulation of 150,000 and a regional paper with 5,600 copies distributed.

The media in Zimbabwe are directed by the Mass Media Trust only in terms of overall editorial policy. The Trust does not interfere with the day-to-day operations of the newspapers, making press freedom possible in Zimbabwe. No member of the Trust has direct oversight of editorial decisions and operations. In effect, the media institutions are self-monitoring and independent.

zimbabwe broadcasting corporation

The objective of ZBC is to provide electronic media service to the people of Zimbabwe. Television provides a national color service. Radio has four fully functioning stations which cover the entire country.

The programming on television has undergone an overhaul since independence and is still undergoing change. Because the television programs do not meet the demands of the audience, they have failed to attract more viewers. Locally originated programming may be one of the ways to increase the audience. In 1982 an independent assessment of television concluded that presentation, like programming, still had a relatively inexperienced technical crew. The television production crews in Zimbabwe have learned from experience how to develop their own programs based on the indigenous culture.

ZBC remains one of the best run media corporations in Africa. The first director, Taravi Kangai, was committed to making the most out of his professionals. Furthermore, the unification of the radio and television stations meant that the duplication in departments which occurs with regularity throughout Africa would not occur in Zimbabwe. An efficient, well-run ZBC with television and radio programming for the entire nation would require trained personnel. The Zimbabwe Institute for Mass Communication was designed to supply trained people both to the Mass Media Trust and ZBC. More than sixty journalists were trained during the first year of operation. They became reporters and media managers in both print and electronic media. Every indication from the initial success of ZBC is that the Zimbabwe Institute for Mass Communication is living up to its objective of supplying the national need for journalists.

eight

ACCESS TO INTERNATIONAL INFORMATION

foreign news agencies

WILCOX (1975, 105) and others believe that "the government ownership and control is so pervasive in many Black African nations" that foreign media serve as one non-governmental source of information. However, such media are hardly independent. Schiller (1976, 37–39) points out that the American media often follows American corporate interests. In effect, the media support the corporate enterprise by producing consumers in the host nations. Most nations in Africa are caught up in a communication system whose rationale is strictly dictated by the Western industrialized nations.

There are several important news agencies which help to mold information in and for the African world: United Press International, Associated Press, Reuters, and Agence-France Presse. As far as Africa is concerned, Reuters and Agence-France Presse are the main foreign agencies. They have bureaus in most capitals of Africa, a legacy of their colonial experience.

Throughout Africa the bureaus of the Agence-France Presse and Reuters are run by national bureau chiefs who are French or English. It is rare when the bureau chief in an African country is an African; most often the bureau heads are citizens of the headquarter countries. As such, the agency operates in an African country with little regard for the well-being of the African country; information is meant to be sold in the home market first. The by-product, that is, sales of a certain piece of information, commodity to other countries and media institutions becomes secondary. The aim is to outdo the competition, where there is competition, in the home market.

Historical relations imposed by the colonial powers on Africa have meant that two agencies dominate the flow of news from Africa to the rest of the world and sometimes between African countries themselves. In addition, of the foreign news coming into Africa, about 93% of it is controlled by Reuters and Agence-France Presse. Information-dependence is an endemic disease in most of Africa. This remains so despite the very remarkable efforts of Alfred Opubor, Paul Ansah and Peter Mwaura among others, to see the establishment of an African news agency located in Dakar, Senegal.

There are several practices of transnational news agencies which are considered injurious to the national interests of African nations. According to the editor of the *Sunday Times* of Zimbabwe, Willie Musururwa, foreign correspondents accredited to Zimbabwe were addicted to the term "tribal" to explain almost everything. Whenever foreign correspondents reported on the two principal political parties in Zimbabwe, ZANU (PF) and ZAPU, there seemed to be a "tribal" analysis, one party being classed as Shona and the other as Ndebele. Musururwa considered this shallow journalism (Musururwa, Dec. 19, 1981). No one would bring up the ethnic category of the various parties in England or the United States of America or Canada, although if one looked hard enough, one might be able to find patterns of ethnic voting. Another practice which seems to irritate African leaders is the foreign correspondents' use of stigmatizing labels for those who are trying to change the repressive political and economic systems of the continent. Many African leaders have at one time or another been called agitators, terrorists, or guerillas. Normality exists only from the standpoint of the

EIGHT

"structure" supported by the news agency. Thus, prior to his overwhelming election by the people of Zimbabwe, Prime Minister Robert Mugabe was called a "marxist terrorist," "communist terrorist" and "militant marxist terrorist." After his election when he appeared on television to speak, few people even within Zimbabwe could believe that the man speaking so cooly, eloquently and rationally was the one that had been labelled by such stigmatizing terms. The foreign news agencies distorted the reality by preconditioning events for their readers. Finally, some foreign correspondents are guilty of over-emphasizing stories in order to have a story. The case of the Karamoja is illustrative. Throughout 1980 and 1981, there was a continuing drama in the northeastern region of Uganda where the Karamajong people lived. There had been a drought and many people had died. A host of journalists from all of the news agencies rushed the three hours by road from Kampala to see the children with distended stomachs and to take photographs of women crying in the refugee camps. This was a dramatic story of hunger and death in Africa. In reality, Uganda is one of the most fertile countries in Africa and no reporter wrote anything about the anomaly of the situation in the Karamoja Province. When people did not seem to die fast enough to make a story, the foreign correspondents reported on the difficulty of the food aid reaching the area due to a tie-up of transport in Kampala. Without a question, there was a story in Karamoja but after the initial reports the story was that so many journalists ate breakfast in their hotels and then travelled out to Karamoja by noon and came back to Kampala to file their cables to London, Paris and New York where people wanted to hear of starving people way off in some barren area of "darkest Africa" and where their journalists had braved the wilds to obtain this story just for them.

Transnational news agencies have been relatively free to operate in Africa despite the appearance of the abuse of the privilege to cable news from the host country in some instances. Foreign correspondents are human and their own prejudices and opinions often enter their cables by what they choose to report as well as how they treat the subject. A minor story of adultery committed by a white farmer and the black wife of one of the farmer's workers was cabled throughout the world by Agence-France Presse and Reuters, finding its way into numerous European newspapers as well as the *New York Times-Washington Post's* international *Herald Tribune*. Yet, almost no African nation imposes restrictions on foreign journalists. No special visa requirements are necessary for the foreign correspondents of the major transnational or national agencies. Once the journalist has a story to file, he or she is free to cable it without interference from government authorities. This remains the case in Marxist nations such as Ethiopia and Angola as well as pro-Western nations such as Sudan and Nigeria, although it would be incorrect to say that African governments are insensitive to negative reporting about their countries. The Congo and Guinea, two traditional socialist states have periodically required a review of cables sent overseas by foreign correspondents.

Governments which have risen to power by military coups are normally more sensitive to foreign correspondents than democratically elected governments, whether socialist or capitalist. General Yakubu Gowon decreed in 1967, soon after his ascendancy to leadership, that no foreign correspondent should relay anything which could be considered damaging to Nigeria. President Mobutu Sese Seku of Zaire, the late Sergeant Samuel Doe of Liberia and Flight Lieutenant Jerry Rawlings of Ghana, have exhibited some apprehension about foreign news correspondents in the past. However, few of them have ever institutionalized cable censorship. When General Obasanjo of Nigeria came to power after the assassination of Murtala Mohammed, he dispensed with the restrictions on foreign correspondents placed in effect by General Gowon. President Shagari's government continued the policy of freedom for foreign correspondents to cable news to their home countries. In 1977, it was estimated that 85% of the African nations had no official policy on reviewing foreign correspondents cables (Wilcox 1975, 115). In actual numbers, of thirty-four nations covered in Wilcox's survey, three required foreign journalists to submit cables. Two others were listed under the category of "insufficient information." Africa remains relatively free of censorship of foreign correspondents and some African leaders such as President Robert Mugabe and former President Julius Nyerere hold or held periodic news conferences for the foreign press.

There are cases of the expulsion of journalists thought to be detrimental to the host African nation. Correspondents of Agence-France Presse have been expelled from several countries including Chad, Central African Republic, Uganda, Zaire, Somalia and the Congo. Expulsion appears to be a way of censoring the foreign news agency without actually making a policy requiring the reviewing of cables. Societies which regularly expel journalists place a burden on the remaining journalists to censor themselves. Among the nations which have expelled journalists of Reuters and Associated Press are Kenya, Malawi and South Africa. The latter nation has also detained journalists without trial. After the prison death in February 1982 of Dr. Neil Aggett, the first white and the forty-first victim of death in detention in South Africa, several foreign journalists were placed under surveillance. A British journalist had been detained a few weeks earlier and then released and expelled from the country. In late 1981, Cynthia Stevens of the Associated Press was expelled from South Africa. Prior to independence in Zimbabwe and under the Ian Smith regime, a number of journalists were expelled form the country. The most celebrated case was that of Peter Niesewand of *The Guardian*. While technically not a correspondent for an international news agency, Niesewand became a symbol of the ruthlessness with which the Rhodesians handled any journalist who did not write what they thought should be written.

in-flow of news

The formulation of policy regarding the in-flow and out-flow of news into African nations demands action at various levels of the governments concerned. More than likely the decision to enter into exclusive contractual agreements for foreign news with some transnational news agencies will be determined by economic factors rather than any attempt to restrict news within the society. Of course, the results will be the same, people will have to depend on what the government decides the newspapers need to publish.

Most African nations have exclusive contracts with a foreign news agency which means that all in-coming news is screened by the national news agency, if one exists, or the Ministry of Information and then sent to the newspapers and radio in the nation. The foreign agency, in these cases, is prohibited from selling news directly to the press.

International news is a commodity and is sold on the market to various African nations by the foreign news agencies. Since individual newspapers can hardly afford to purchase the services of the foreign news agencies, the government buys and distributes the news to newspapers at a lower cost than what the government pays.

Poorer nations such as Chad, Upper Volta, Ghana, Botswana, Guinea and Niger normally have exclusive contracts in order to save foreign currency. Even relatively "rich" countries such as Zimbabwe and the Ivory Coast have had to curtail the distribution of certain periodicals, not in an attempt to control the press but rather to conserve foreign currency. Similarly, the exclusive contractual agreements mean that only one price is paid for the news to the foreign agency even though several domestic news services may make use of the information.

Normally national news agencies handle the in-coming news. Some of the agencies are little more than a director and a secretary in a small office within some larger ministry. The purpose of these agencies may range from screening and filtering to merely relaying the news to national outlets. There are numerous models for handling in-coming news. Taking Zimbabwe as an example, there are two conduits for in-coming news: ZIANA and Zimbabwe Broadcasting Corporation (ZBC). ZIANA has contracts with Reuters and Associated Press. Everything which enters the country from those two services is seen and distributed to the local press by ZIANA. On the other hand, Agence-France Presse has its contract with the Zimbabwe Broadcasting Corporation. The difference in conduits for in-coming news in Zimbabwe has its roots in historical circumstances. Reuters and Associated Press operated bureaus under the Ian Smith regime and consequently were able to secure contracts with the South African Press Association (SAPA) which preceded ZIANA as the domestic news agency in the country. Agence-France Presse as a latecomer arranged its contract with ZBC during the transition from the Smith-Muzorewa era to the Mugabe government. The Ministry of

EIGHT

Foreign Affairs receives its own printouts of all agencies' in-coming news. Under the leadership of Dr. Davison Sadza, the Zimbabwe Mass Media Trust has undertaken to rectify the anomaly in the channels for in-coming news. One contract for a foreign agency through one national agency seems to be the kind of economic symmetry for which most African nations strive in order to conserve foreign currency. Wilf Mbanga, former acting director of ZIANA says "we believe that ZIANA should become the principal conduit for every foreign agency seeking to supply news to Zimbabwe" (Personal interview, February 10, 1982). Many African nations have moved to make their own news gathering agencies responsive to all the news that enters or wants to enter their borders. The Tunis Afrique Press (TAP) of Tunisia, the Algerie Presse Service (APS), The News Agency of Nigeria (NAN), and The Jamahiriyah Arab Revolutionary News Agency (ARNA) of Libya have made their agencies responsible for serving as conduits to all foreign services seeking to supply them with news.

PAN AFRICAN NEWS AGENCY (PANA)

A VISION

Kwame Nkrumah becomes more legendary as a visionary the farther his life recedes into the past. In 1957 when Ghana became independent, Nkrumah, its first president, envisioned a united Africa with Ghana leading the way. Fresh from his political campaigning, imbued with the doctrines of Marcus Garvey, W.E.B. Du Bois and C.L.R. James, Kwame Nkrumah proposed the Organization of African Unity. Along with this organization, he proposed an All-African news agency (Barton 1979, 26). He neither remained at the helm of Ghana nor lived so long as to see the formation of his dream. Like many of his proposals, all relating to the greater glory of Africa, the All-African News Agency has finally caught on among Africans who were school boys and girls when Nkrumah was generating ideas for the resurrection of Africa.

The realization of the Pan African News Agency (PANA) is a testament to Nkrumah's visions. Amadou M'Bow, former Director-General of UNESCO, was one of the principal architects of the news agency. He saw the need for Africans to report the news about Africa because of the partisan selection of news and choice of words in the transnational agencies files. A. Marere (1982), the former Executive Secretary of the Zimbabwe Mass Media Trust, has put it this way: "The transnationals serve their constituents and they serve them well for what they want to read but they do not serve us well." A similar line is taken by almost every leader of an African news agency. The largest and most viable independent agency in Africa is now News Agency of Nigeria (NAN) which succeeded Ghana News Agency as the most efficient in Africa. The decline of Ghana's political and economic fortunes led to the critical drawing in of the reins of what could have been a very dynamic agency. The creation of PANA became a necessity in the early 1980's. African leaders gave the impetus to a movement that had been dreamed about by the late Kwame Nkrumah. In fact, Nkrumah had remarked at the 1965 dedication of the Ghana News Agency that, "We see right and wrong, just and unjust, progressive and reactionary, positive and negative, friend and foe. We are partisan" (*The Spark*, October 1, 1965). Nkrumah wanted a new type of journalist who would fill the pages of the newspapers with "a clear ideology of the African Revolution." He concluded:

> The drum beat of the African Revolution must throb in the pages of his newspapers and magazines, it must sound in the voices and feelings of our news readers. To this end, we need a new kind of journalist of the African Revolution (*Ibid.*).

The logic of necessity had made the development of a Pan African news agency inevitable by the beginning of 1980. There may have been no more talk about "journalist of the African Revolution" but there was plenty of talk about the need for "an African news agency."

THE CREATION

During the latter half of the twentieth century, media have themselves become a major news story (Rubin 1977, 7). In Africa, the foreign news agencies, particularly the big six—Reuters, UPI, AP, Agence-France Presse,

EIGHT

Tass and Hsinhua—are often the source of much dissatisfaction among African leaders. The enormous capability of these agencies to transmit negative or positive images about an African country is not easily celebrated by emerging nations. A nation's ability to attract investors, tourists, and favorable chronicles is determined in large part by the image the outside world has and, too often, African leaders have argued, the foreign news agencies have created the external images of Africa detrimental to the continent's development. To counter the overwhelming ability of foreign news agencies to dominate the in-flow and out-flow of African news, the African News organizations created the Pan African News Agency in July, 1979 (PANA). It was headquartered at Dakar, Senegal and headed by an attorney, Sheikh Usman Diallo.

PANA set up regional offices in Lusaka, Zambia; Lagos, Nigeria; Khartoum, Sudan; Kinshasa, Zaire; and Tripoli, Libya. The aim of the agency was to cover the entire continent. With the encouragement of Amadou M'Bow, director-General of UNESCO, PANA began to create its infrastructure in 1980. M'Bow, a firm believer in the open flow of communication and the democratization of news flow, was instrumental in getting UNESCO to award PANA two million U.S. dollars for its organization. Member countries were also asked to share in the cost of operations. Although nearly thirty African nations possessed their own news agencies, most could see the value of a Pan-African agency. The regional offices were meant to solidify the OAU's insistence that the agency cover the entire continent.

Goodwill existed on the part of all African nations participating in the setting up of the agency. Nevertheless the pragmatics of establishing an international agency, even in Africa and even where participants seemed to want to cooperate, can present difficulties.

On February 6 and 7, 1982, the board of PANA met in Dakar during the harmattan season to try and clean away the dust surrounding the international tariffs among the nations. A special committee was set up to discuss the role of the varying tariffs in the dissemination of news. This technical committee recommended the reduction in tariffs in order to encourage the free flow of news among African states. Most representatives considered this recommendation favorably although it posed the problem of a reduction in foreign currency exchange derived from the major transnational news agencies.

However, in March, 1982 a meeting of African ministers of information in Dakar, called by the OAU to discuss the remaining issues surrounding the operationalization of PANA, broke down when members of the Polisario Liberation Movements for the Saharawi Republic were not permitted to land at the airport by Senegalese authorities. Led by Algeria, which backed the Polisario, a group of fourteen nations walked out of the meeting, leaving the issue of the Pan African News Agency to be worked out after the knottier issue of political recognition of Polisario was clarified. Morocco's design on the territory, previously called Spanish Sahara, created international antagonisms which threatened to dismantle the easy union of the OAU.

Reciprocal foreign news agreements

Under the auspices of PANA, numerous countries have stepped up their efforts to complete reciprocal foreign news agreements. In May 1982, at Lusaka, Zambia, the regional center for PANA in Southern Africa, a distinguished group of African journalists and information officers met to discuss the best ways to implement the reciprocal agreements.

Inasmuch as most of the nations receive the majority of their international news from extra-continental news agencies, the creation of the African reciprocal news distribution scheme would serve as a base upon which the Pan African News Agency could be established. Although at present nearly seventy-five percent of all African governments hold exclusive contracts with Reuters, Agence-France Presse, United Press International, or TASS, the introduction of the reciprocal scheme will serve to broaden the sources of news for each country. Ownership of the exclusive contracts with transnational agencies underscores the inability of private citizens to afford this service in most nations. Wilcox recognizes that government controls communication contracts but believes that this is a negative situation (Wilcox 1975, 117). Actually, without government purchasing, the news services of most nations would be poorer. As it is, some nations, such as Somalia and Tanzania, have found it difficult to maintain the payments on such services and they have been periodically suspended.

As the reciprocal agreements are effected, such as the one between Shihata of Tanzania and ZIANA of Zimbabwe, they will provide for the reciprocal posting of news via TELEX and the post to each country. The agency sending the information will be responsible for postage costs. There is no plan to locate journalists from either country in the other country. All news will be disseminated by the regular news collection and distribution personnel of the agency. This will of course reduce expenses.

Shihata and ZIANA will send stories to each other every day and consequently the news coming directly from the two nations without a third party, e.g., Reuters, will reduce cost greatly. However, one of the problems which will remain, even after an effective continental reciprocal program, is the dependence on the transnational for news about the Americas, Europe, and Asia. Clearly the reciprocal agreement scheme does not solve the problem of receiving information about the Argentina-Britain War in the South Atlantic or the Mideast Israeli-Arab confrontation or the election of an African-American to a high political post in the United States of America. To receive this news the agencies will have to depend on the historically strong Western agencies or Cable News Network (CNN) which is quickly becoming a global news network.

Another problem which the reciprocal agreements have to avoid is the redistribution of transnational agency news. It becomes an attractive device for some agencies, although it is technically illegal, to put their mark or modifications on a story and ship it out. If this happened, the purpose of the reciprocals will be defeated and the information sought regarding a nation will be basically from the same Western source as before.

There is promise for continental dissemination in this scheme because it utilizes the present resources of the national information institutions. Without having to post correspondents to the various nations around Africa, the newspapers and agencies of a country can receive news from a regular reporter who is a national of the originating nation. Such news is likely to be more educational, more positive, and more sympathetic to the originating nation. African nations would be able to learn about successful agricultural projects in neighboring nations, appreciate the culture of other nations, or rejoice in their triumph and be sad in their failures as occupiers of the same continent. Such positive developments were being encouraged by UNESCO during the M'Bow administration. The Sean McBride Commission of 1979 went a long way toward opening up new avenues for dissemination innovations. A. Marere said in Lusaka at the regional PANA meeting in June, 1982 that, "PANA offers the best hope of consolidating Africa's place in the framework of international communication." Marere's insistence that reciprocity be a part of the groundwork for PANA was widely applauded.

NINE

THE MEDIA AND IDEOLOGY
A FINAL NOTE

IDEOLOGY REFERS to a system of ideas used as a blueprint to achieve certain political, social or economic objectives. Numerous African nations design "five-year plans" along the lines of socialist states in order to direct their national energies toward the fulfillment of socio-economic goals. According to Mannheim, ideology is the conservative justification of the status quo and Utopia is the creative outlook that wants to change reality (Mannheim 1972). It appears that many African nations are victims of ideology; they have allowed their thinking about media issues to be entirely encapsulated by inflexible ideological postures. Thus, new political experience and new socio-economic realities are disavowed. Since all ideologies depend, for a time, on prejudices and cliches, an ideological approach to media must be cautious. The ideological orientations of African states affect how those states utilize the media, structure the media, and train media specialists. Two predominant modes of economic thought exist in contemporary Africa: capitalist ideology and socialist ideology. Even states such as Tanzania and Kenya which take a non-aligned posture are in effect socialist or capitalist in orientation.

THE MEDIA AND IDEOLOGY

States purporting to be capitalist in orientation, for example, Nigeria and Ivory Coast, utilize the media as handmaids of the industrial order. Advertisements and commercials are welcomed on the TV stations as sponsors of programs. A profit orientation allows these nations to invest in program development and experimentation. The direction of their program and experimentation efforts tend to be Western. Nigeria, for example, contracted an African-American firm, led by the television news journalist Randy Daniels, to help improve television programming and on-the-air presentation. Such a business transaction is less likely among the socialist oriented states where the leaning is toward socialist industrialized nations, none of which have any substantial populations of African origin. The African states who trade in services and goods with the United States are also more likely to trade with other blacks because of the presence of African-American entrepreneurs. In many nations however, African-Americans are looked upon simply as Americans.

Most African nations, including those which have adopted a capitalist orientation have, a centrist philosophy regarding the media, especially the electronic media. The concentration of power in a strong central administration is typical. In such systems, financial support is largely the responsibility of the government. There has, however, been a rapid development of commercial advertising on television in countries like Nigeria, Kenya, and the Ivory Coast.

Although newspapers have traditionally accepted advertisements from the public even in socialist oriented nations like Tanzania, Mozambique, Angola, and Ethiopia, television in the socialist countries where it exists has tried to minimize commercial advertisements. Tirivafi Kangai of the Zimbabwe Broadcasting Corporation said in an interview in February, 1982 that the ZTV was attempting to minimize the reliance on commercials because they represented all of the worst values of a capitalist state which the government had rejected.

The capitalist model, where media survive and expand because of advertising revenue, is being adapted in some African nations. Socialist nations reject this approach to media growth contending that wealthy

NINE

businessmen can control the content of the media because of the heavy reliance on support from their advertisements. The capitalists argue that government control of the purse strings makes the media the voice of the government. In the free enterprise systems, they argue, the media institutions will have more than one master and by virtue of the diversity and disparity between them not have to serve any private interest, thus remaining essentially free of external control.

Financial support for television and print journalism in socialist African nations is not dependent upon market demands. Programs for television and radio may be aired and continue on the air despite a lack of consumer appeal. The greater control there is in a society, the less is media support dependent on the consumer (Cassata & Asante 1979, 53). One reason for Nigeria hiring the African-American television consultants was because they wanted their programming to appeal to consumers. The more appeal, the better the advertising money. To be sure, there are abuses of the commercial system in media. The best media organizations have long histories of the rejection of certain advertising for airing. Not everything is accepted for broadcasting. The media organization, working within the limits of its own principles and standards should reject advertisements in poor taste. The Radio Code and the Television Code of the United States state clearly that broadcasters should, in recognition of their responsibility to the public, refuse the facilities of their stations to an advertiser where they have good reason to doubt the integrity of the advertiser, the truth of the advertising representations, or the compliance of the advertiser with the spirit and purpose of all applicable legal requirements. Many African nations operate with a clear set of codes governing the media. Each nation, out of its own historical context, must develop its own standards of operation.

Freedom and Responsibility

Although media are present in many areas of Africa, millions of people still have little access to the written word or electronic media. Those nations that have managed to communicate through print and electronic media with large masses of their people have often thrust upon their journalists the sharp

THE MEDIA AND IDEOLOGY

agony of choosing between freedom and responsibility. This is not the case in every nation, nor perhaps, in most but yet the burdens of a censored press, harassed reporters and threatened media specialists have to be borne by many communicationists in Africa.

The journalist, whether managing editor or reporter, has many responsibilities to his or her county, staff, the organization, but above all to the readers and viewers. Public interest is best served in Africa, as elsewhere, when the public is fully informed of all facts and circumstances which might affect how they view reality. Faced with the cruel fact of forced closing or censorship, the media specialist in Africa must often choose between self-censorship and complete shut-down, and frequently not because of ideological differences, though often enough that is the case, but primarily for exposing some government irregularity. Such criticism is considered to be anti-government although it may be, and often is, pro-people. Editors will often try to justify their self-censorship by using the letters to the editor as a means of hinting at the lurking truth. To defy the authority of the state and make a bold declaration will sometimes leave the nation without a voice. Donald Woods was faced with this type of dilemma in South Africa. The South African authorities attacked him for his outspoken stance against apartheid. Woods was born in South Africa, studied law in Capetown and became a journalist. At 31, he was made editor of the **Daily Dispatch**, once a leading apartheid newspaper. Until he was silenced by a banning order in October, 1977, he was the most widely read white columnist in South Africa.

Edgar Mahlomolo Motuba was editor of the *Leselinyana* in Lesotho. His paper never ceased to attack the corruption and injustice in his country. Although Motuba was warned to discontinue his exposure of injustice in Lesotho, he refused to keep silent. In September, 1981, he was attacked and killed by assailants. This is an example of an extreme case of censorship.

There is a very thin line between government restraint and government censorship. Since 75% of the printing presses in the 32 African countries that restrain the media are owned by the government, it is rather easy for the government to determine the limits of a journalist's freedom. Because of foreign exchange difficulties many nations regulate newsprint when it is imported, thereby creating another measure for indirect restraint.

In Sudan, membership of the government party is an essential qualification to obtain a license to be a journalist (J. Spicer 1982, 10). Such requirements make it unlikely that anyone who holds different views from the government would ever be considered qualified to be a journalist. The hard fact is that **survival** and **stability** are main calling cards of African governments in the contemporary international sphere; consequently there is a tendency toward centralization and consolidation of power, political and informational, close to the ruling circles. In many ways, ideologies are merely the convenient hat-racks for governments to hang their less than subtle as well as their subtle attacks on the press. Freedom and responsibility are organic in their relationship in African media and must be nourished by a healthy environment.

conclusion

The voice of the media in Africa, as can be seem by our discussion, is often loud and clear. At other times, too many times, it is a weak and ineffectual voice. There will need to be an entire generation of African communicationists and working journalists committed to engaging their nations in the most far-reaching activities of the media experience. These will be intelligent, courageous, and patriotic journalists, not unlike the hundreds of men and women who have made African journalism productive in the face of numerous difficulties.

Actually those individuals are already rising from the political battles in their own countries with renewed vigor for a voice of power. This means that development communication, so close to the political agendas of African nations, will have to be defined in ways that leave the journalists unrestrained and capable of the thundering realities of the people's social, cultural, and political lives. Our faith, because we have witnessed so much wit, ingenuity and flexibility in African journalists is that the first words have already been sent by Shango's mighty voice.

appendix A

THE LEADING MEDIA INSTITUTIONS IN AFRICA

	Daily Press	Radio and Television	News Agency
ALGERIA	*Ach-cha'ab* 1 Place Maurice Audin Algiers F. 1962 *Horizons* 20 Rue de la Liberte Algiers F. 1985 *Al-Joumhouria* 6 Rue ben Senoussi Oran F. 1963 *Al-Massa* Algiers F. 1985	*Radiodiffusion* *Television* *Algerienne* *(RTA)* 21 Blvd des Martyrs Algiers	*Algerie Press* *Service (APS)* 7 Blvd. Che Guevara Algiers F. 1962

* = weekly; ** = twice weekly

APPENDIX A

(ALGERIA)	*Al-Moudjahid* 20 Rue de la Liberte Algiers F. 1965		
	An-Nasr BP 388 Constantine F. 1963		
ANGOLA	*Diaro da Republica* Caixa Postal 1306 Luanda	*Televisao Popular de Angola* Caixa Postal 2604 Luanda	ANGOP Luanda
	A Jornal de Angola Caixa Postal 1312 Luanda F. 1923	*Radio Nacional de Angola* Caixa Postal 1329 Luanda	
BENIN	*L'aube Nouvelle* Cotonou	*Office de Radiodiffusion et Television du Benin* BP 366, Cotonou	Agence Benin-Presse (ABP) Cotonou
	Bullentin de L'Agence Benin-Presse Cotonou		
	Ehuzu BP 1210 Cotonou	*La Voix de la Revolution* BP 366, Cotonou	
BOTSWANA	*Daily News* P.O.B. 51 Gaborne F. 1964	*Radio Botswana* Private Bag 0060 Gaborone	

THE LEADING MEDIA INSTITUTIONS IN AFRICA

BURKINA FASO	*Notre Combat* BP 584, Ouagadougou	*La Voix du Renouveau* BP 511, Ouagadougou	
BURUNDI	*Le Renouveau de Burundi* Ministry of Information BP 2870 Bujumbura F. 1978	*Voix de la Revolution* BP 1900 Bujumbura	Agence burundaise de Presse (ABP) BP 2870 Bujumbura
CAMEROON	*Cameroon Tribune* BP 1218 Yaounde F. 1974	*CRTV Office de Radiodiffusion Television Camerounnaise* Yaounde	*Societe Publicite Edition Du Cameroon* (SOPECAM) BP 1218 Yaounde
CAPE VERDE	**Vox di Povo* Praia, Sao Tiago Boletin Official	*Emissora Official da Republica de Cabo Verde* CP 26 Sao Tiago *Radio Nacional de Cabo Verde* Praca *Voz de Sao Vicente* CP 29, Mindelo Sao Vicente, F. 1974	Agence France-Presse (AFP) CP 26118 Praia Interpress Service (IPS) Italy

APPENDIX A

(CAPE VERDE)		*Televisao Experimental de Cabo Verde (TEVEC)* Achado de Santo Antonio, CP 2 Praio, Sao Tiago	
CENTRAL AFRICAN REPUBLIC	*El Le Songo* Bangui	*Radiodiffusion-Television* Centrafrique BP 940 Bangui	Agence Centrafique de Presse (ACAP) BP 40 Bangui
CHAD	*Infor-tchad* BP 670 N'Djamena	*Radiodiffusion Nationale tchadienne* BP 892 N'Djamena	Agence Tchadienne du Presse (ATP) BP 670 N'Djamena
		Radio Moundo BP 122 Moundo	
COMOROS		*Radio-Camoros* BP 250 Moroni	Agence Comores Presse (ACP) Moroni
CONGO	*ACI* BP 2144 Brazzaville	*Radiodiffusion-television National Congolaise* BP 2241 Brazzaville	Angence Congolaise d'Information (ACI) BP 2144 Brazzaville
	L'Eveil de Pointe Noire BP 66 Pointe Noire		

THE LEADING MEDIA INSTITUTIONS IN AFRICA

(CONGO)	M Weti BP 991 Brazzaville	La Voix de la Revolution Congolaise BP 2241 Brazzaville	
		Television Nationale Congolaise BP 2241 Brazzaville	
DJIBOUTI	*Le Reveil de Djibouti BP 268 Djibouti	Radiodiffucion- Television de Djibouti BP 97 Djibouti	Agence Djiboutienne de Presse (ADP) BP 32 Djibouti
EGYPT	Barad ach- ChariKat POB 813 Alexandria F. 1952	Egyptian Radio & Television Corp. (ERTV) POB 1186 Cairo F. 1928	Middle East News Agency 4 Sharia Hoda Sharawi Cairo F. 1955
	Al-Ittihad al- Misri 13 Sharia Sidi Abd ar-Razzak Alexandria F. 1871	Middle East Radio 24-26 Sharia ZaVaria Ahmad Cairo F. 1964	
	Le Journal d'Alexdrie 1 Sharia Rolo Alexandria	Egyptian Television Organization POB 1186 Cairo F. 1960	

APPENDIX A

(EGYPT)
La Reforme
8 passage sherif
Alexandria
F. 1985

As-Safeer
4 Sharia as-
Sahafa
Alexandria
F. 1924

Tachydromos-
Egyptos
4 Sharia Zan-
garol
Alexandria
F. 1879

EQUATORIAL GUINEA
Ebano
Malabo

Radio Ecuatorial
Apdo. 749
Bata

Radio Sante
Isabel, Apdo
195, Malabo

Africa 2000
Malabo F. 1988

ETHIOPIA
Addis Zemen
POB 30145
Addis Ababa
F. 1941

Ethiopian Herald
POB 30701
Addis Ababa
F. 1943

Voice of Ethiopia
POB 1020
Addis Ababa

Ethiopian
Television
POB 5544
Addis Ababa

Ethiopian News
Agency (ENA)
POB 530
Addis Ababa

THE LEADING MEDIA INSTITUTIONS IN AFRICA

(ETHIOPIA)	*Hibret* POB 247 Asmara Tigrinya		
GABON	*Gabon-matin* BP 168 Libreville	*Radiodiffusion- Television Gabonaise* BP 150 Libreville	Agence Gabonaise de Presse BP 168 Libreville
	L'Union BP 3849 Libreville F. 1975	*Tele Africa* Libreville	
GAMBIA	*Gambia Outlook* Banjul	*Radio Gambia* Mile 7, Banjul	
	The Gambian 60 Lancaster St., Banjul		
GHANA	*Daily Graphic* POB 742 Accra F. 1950	*Ghana Broadcasting Corp.* POB 1633 Accra F. 1935	Ghana News Agency POB 2118 Accra F. 1957
	Ghanaian Times POB 2638 Accra F. 1958		
	People's Evening News POB 7505 Accra		
	The Pioneer POB 325 Accra		

APPENDIX A

GUINEA	*Horoya BP 191 Conarky	Radiodiffusion Nationale de Guinee BP 391 Conakry	Agence Guine- enne de Presse BP 1535 Conakry
GUINEA- BISSAU	No Pintcha Bissau 1990 Voz da Guine Bissau	Radiodiffusion Nacional da Republica da Guine-Bissau CP 191 Bissau	Agencia No- ticiosa da Guin- ea (ANG) CP 248 Bissau
IVORY COAST	Fraternite-Matin BP 1807 Abidjan	Radiodiffusion Ivoirienne BP V191 Abidjan Television Iviorienne BP 8883 Abidjan	Agence Ivoiri- enne de Presse (AIP) BP 4312 Abidjan
KENYA	Daily Nation POB 49010 Nairobi F. 1960 Kenya Leo POB 30958 Nairobi Kenya Times POB 30958 Nairobi The Standard POB 30080 Nairobi F. 1960	Voice of Kenya POB 30456 Nairobi Kenya Broad- casting (KBC) POB 30456 Nairobi	Kenya News Agency POB 8053 Nairobi

(KENYA)   *Taifa Leo*
          POB 49010
          Nairobi
          F. 1960

LESOTHO   *Lesotho National*   Lesotho News
                                 Broadcasting   Agency (LSNA)
                                 Service   POB 36
                                 POB 552   Maseru (1983)
                                 Maseru 100

LIBERIA   *Daily Observer*   *ELBC*   Liberian News
          117 Broad St.   POB 594   Agency (LINA)
          POB 1858   Monrovia F.   POB 9021
          Monrovia F.   1960   Capitol Hill
          1981   Monrovia

                                 ELBC: Liberian
                                 Broadcasting
                                 System, POB
                                 594
                                 Monrovia

                                 Lamco Broadcast-
                                 ing Station
                                 (EINR)
                                 Nimba

                                 Liberia Rural
                                 Communications
                                 Network
                                 POB 2176
                                 Monrovia

                                 Radio ELWA
                                 POB 192
                                 Monrovia

APPENDIX A

(LIBERIA)		Voice of America Monrovia	
		ELTV: Liberian Broadcasting System POB 594 Monrovia	
LIBYA	Al-Fajr al-Jadid POB 2303 Tripoli F. 1969	Great Sociolist People's Libyan Arab Jamahiriya Broadcasting POB 3731 Tripoli F. 1957	Jamahiriya News Agency (JANA) POB 2303
MADA- GASCAR	*Bulletin de l'Agence Na- tionale, d' Infor- mation Taratra (Anta)* BP 386 Antananarivo *Heby* BP 1648 Atananarivo F. 1949 *Imongo Vaovao* 11-k4 bis An- dravoahangy Atananarivo *Madagascar Tribune* 101 Antanarivo	*Radiodiffusion Television Malgache* BP 442 Atananarivo	Agence Nationale D'Information (ANTA) PB 386 Atananarivo

(MADA-GASCAR)	*Midi-Madagascar* BP 1414 Ankorondrano		
	Maresaka 12 Lelana Ratsima John, Isotry 101 Antananoriva 1953		
MALAWI	*The Daily Times* PB 39, Ginnery Corner Blantyre F. 1895	*Malawi Broadcasting Corp.* POB 30133 Chichiri Blantyre	Malawi News Agency (MANA) Mzuza
MALI	*Bulletin Quoudien de la Chambre de Commerce et d'Industrie du Mali* BP 46 Bamako	*Radiodiffusion Television Maliene* BP 171 Bamako F. 1957	Agence Malienne de Presse et Promotion (AMAP) BP 116 Bamako F. 1977
	L'Essor-La Voix du Peuple BP 141 Bamako		
MAURITANIA	*Ach-Chaab* BP 371 Nouakchott	*Office de Radiodiffusion et Television de Mauritanie (ORTM)* BP 200 Nouakchott 1958	Agence Mauritanienne de l'Information (AMI) BP 371 Nouakchott

APPENDIX A

MAURITIUS

China Times
Emmanuel
Anquetil St.
POB 325
Port Louis
1953

Chinese Daily News
32 Remy Ollier Street
Port Louis
F. 1932

L'Express
3 Brown Sequard St.
Port Louis
F. 1963

La Socialiste
3rd Floor
Marilall Bldg.
Port Louis

Le Mauricien
8 St. Georges St., POB 7
Port Louis
F. 1908

The New Nation
31 Edith Cavell St., POB 7
Port Louis
F. 1971

Mauritius Broadcasting Corp.
Broadcasting House
Louis Pasteur Street
Port Louis

Mauritus Broadcasting Corporation
Broadcasting House
Louis Pasteur St. Forest Side
F. 1964

(MAURITIUS) *The Sun*
31 Edith Cavell St.
Port Louis

MOROCCO *Al-Bayane*
BP 13152
Casablanca

Al-Ittihad al-Ichtiraki
33 Rue Emir Abdelkader
Casablanca

Maroc Soir
34 Rue Muhammad Smiha
Casablanca

Le Matin du Sahara
34 Rue Muhammad Smiha
Casablanca

Rissalat al-Oumma
158 Ave. des Forces Armees Royales
Casablanca

Al-Alam
BP 141
Rabat F. 1946

Radiodiffusion Television Marocaine
BP 1042
Rabat F. 1962

2 M International
52 Ave Hassan II
Casablanca F. 1988

Radio Mediterranee Internationale
BP 2055
Tangier

Voice of America Radio Station in Tangier
U.S. Consulate General
Tangier

Wikalat al-Maghreb al-Arabi (WMA)
BP 1049
Rabat F. 1959

APPENDIX A

(MOROCCO) *Al-Anba's*
21 Rue Patrice
Lumumba
Rabat F. 1970

Al-Maghrib
6 Rue Laos
Rabat F. 1970
Tangier

Al-Mithaq al-Watari
6 Rue Laos
Rabat F. 1977

An-Nidal Ad-Bimokrati
18 Rue Tunis
Rabat

L'Opinion
11 Ave Allal
Ben Abdallah
Rabat

MOZAM- *Diario de*   *Radio Mocam-*   Agencia de
BIQUE   *Mocambique*   *bique*   Informacao de
        CP 81   CP 2000   Macambique
        Beira   Maputo F. 1975   (AIM)
                                                CP 896
        Noticias   *Televisao Experi-* Maputo
        CP 327   *mental (TVE)*
        Maputo F. 1926   CP 2675
                            Maputo F. 1981

THE LEADING MEDIA INSTITUTIONS IN AFRICA

NAMIBIA	*Allegmeine Zeitung* POB 56 Windhoek F. 1915	*Nambia Broadcasting Corporation* POB 321 Windhoek 9000	
	Die Republikein POB 3436 Windhoek 9000		
	Windhoek Advertiser POB 56 Windhoek F. 1919		
NIGER	*La Sahel* BP 368 Niamey F. 1960	*"La Voix du Sahel"* BP 361 Niami	Agence Nigerienne de Presse (ANP) BP 11158 Niamey
		Office de Radiodiffusione-Television du Niger (ORTN) BP 309 Niamey	
		Tele-Sahel BP 309 Niamey	
NIGERIA	*Amana* POB 4483 Lagos	*Federal Radio Corp.* Broadcasting House PMB 12504 Lagos	News Agency of Nigeria Lagos

145

APPENDIX A

(NIGERIA)

Daily Express
5-11 Apongbon
Lagos

Daily Sketch
PMB 5067
Ibadan F. 1964

Daily Star
PMB 1139
Enugn

Daily Times
3-7 Kakawa
Lagos F. 1925

Evening Star
PMB 1139
Enugu

Evening Times
PMB 21340
Lagos

The Guardian
PMB 1217
Lagos

Imole Owuro
PMB 5239
Ibadan

Isokan
POB 4483
Lagos

Nigerian Television Authority (NTA)
PMB 12036
Lagos

(NTA)
Aba/Owerri
PMB 7126
Aba

NTA
Abeokuta
PMB 2190
Abeokuta

NTA
Abuja
Abuja

NTA
Akure
PMB 794
Akure

NTA
Bauchi
PBM 0146
Bauchi

NTA
Benin City
PMB 1117
Benin City

146

(NIGERIA)

National Concord
POB 4483
42 Concord Way
Ikeja, Lagos
F. 1980

New Democrat
POB 4457
Kudana South
F. 1983

New Nigerian
POB 254
Kaduna F. 1965

Nigerian Chronicle
POB 1074
Calabur
F. 1970

Nigerian Herald
PMB 1369
Illorin
F. 1973

Nigerian Mirror
Iweka Rd.
Onitsha

Nigerian Observer
18 Airport Rd.
POB 1143
Benin City
F. 1968

NTA
Calabar
105 Marion Road
Calabar

NTA
Enugu
PMB 01530
Enuga, Anambra State

NTA
Ibadan
POB 1460

NTA
Ikeja
Tejuosho Ave.
Surulere

NTA
Ilorin
PMB 1453
Ilorin

NTA
Jos
PMB 2134
Jos

NTA
Kaduna
POB 1347
Kaduna

APPENDIX A

(NIGERIA)

	Nigerian Standard PMB 2112 Jos	NTA Kano PMB 3343 Kano
	Nigerian Star PMB 73 Port Harcourt	NTA Lagos PMB 12005 Lagos
	Nigerian Statesman POB 1095 Owerri	NTA Maiduguri PMB 1487 Maiduguri
	Nigerian Tide POB 5072 Port Harcourt	NTA Makurdi PMB 2044 Makurdi
	Nigerian Tribune POB 78 Ibadan F. 1980	NTA Minna PMB 79 Minna
	The Punch PMB 21204 Ikeja F. 1976	NTA Port Harcourt PMB 5797 Port Harcourt
	The Renaissance POB 1139 Enugu	NTA Sokoto PMB 2351 Sokoto
	The Triumph PMB 3155 Kano	

(NIGERIA)		*NTA* Yola PMB 2197 Yola	
REUNION	*Journal de L'Ile de la Reunion* BP 98 97463 St. Denis	*France Region 3* Place Sarda Garrida Saint-Denis 97405	
	Quotidien de la Reunion et du L'Ocean Indien BP 303 97467 St. Denis		
	Temoignages BP 192 97465 St. Denis		
RWANDA	*Journal Officiel* BP 15 Kigali	*Deutsche Welle* Relay Station in Kigali Africa	Agence Rwandaise de Presse BP 83, Kigali
	Nouvellesdu Rwanda BP 117 Butare	*Radiodiffusion de la Republique Rwandaise* BP 83 Kigali	
	Revue Pedagogique BP 622 Kigali		
	La Source BP 134 or BP 117 Butare		

APPENDIX A

SAO TOME		*Radio Nacional de Sao Tome e Principe* CP 44 Sao Tome	STP-Press Sao Tome F. 1985
SENEGAL	*Le Soleil* BP 29 Dakar F. 1970	*Office de Radiodiffusion Television du Senegal* BP 1765 or 2375 Dakar	Agence de Presse Senegalaise BP 117 Dakar
SEYCHELLES	*The Seychelles Nation* POB 321 Victoria	*RTS-Radio* POB 321 Victoria *Far East Broadcasting Assoc. (FEBA)* POB 234 Mahe *RTS-TV* POB 321 Mahe	Seychelles Agence de Presse (SAP) POB 321 Victoria
SIERRA LEONE	*Daily Mail* POB 53 Freetown F. 1931	*Sierra Leone Broadcasting Service* New England, Freetown F. 1934	Sierra Leone News Agency (SLENA) Wallace Johnson St. Freetown
SOMALIA	*Xiddigta Oktobar* POB 1178 Mogadishu	*Somalia Broadcasting Service* Mogadishu	Somali National News Agency POB 1748 Mogadishu

(SOMALIA)

Radio Hargeisa
POB 14
Hargeisa

Radio Mogadishu
Mogadishu

SOUTH AFRICA

The Argus
POB 56
Capetown
F. 1857

Cape Times
77 Burg St.
POB 17
Captetown
F. 1876

Daily Dispatch
POB 131
East London

Daily News
POB 1491
Durban F. 1878

Diamond Fields Advertiser
POB 610
Kimberly

Die Burger
POB 692
Cape Town

South African Broadcasting Corporation
PB X1
Auckland Park
2006

SABC-Radio
PB X1
Auckland Park
2006

Radio RSA
POB 91313
Auckland Park
2006

SABC-Television
PB X41
Auckland Park
2006

South African Press Association
POB 7766
Johannesburg
2000

APPENDIX A

(SOUTH AFRICA)

Eastern Province Herald
POB 1117
Port Elizabeth

Evening Post
POB 1121
Port Elizabeth

Oosterlig
POB 525
Port Elizabeth

SUDAN

Al-Ayam
POB 2158
Khartoum F.
1953

Al-Engazal-Watan
Khartoum

Al-Khartoum
Khartoum

Al-Midan
Khartoum

Ar-Rayah
Khartoum

As Sudan al-Hadeeth
Khartoum

Sudan Times
Khartoum

Sudan Broadcasting Service
POB 572
Omdurman

National Radio & Television Corp.
Omdurman

Sudan National Broadcasting Corp.
POB 1094
Omdurman

Sudan News Agency (SUNA)
POB 1506
Khartoum

(SUDAN)	*As-Sudani* Khartoum	
	Ath-Thawra Khartoum	
	Al-Usbu Khartoum	
SWAZILAND	*Times of Swaziland* POB 156 Mbabane F. 1897	*Swaziland Broadcasting & Information Service* POB 338 Mbabane F. 1966
	Swaziland Observer POB A385 Mbabane	*Swaziland Commerical Radio (Pty) Ltd.* POB 23114 Johannesburg 2044
		Swaziland Television Broadcasting POB A146 Mbabane F. 1978
		Trans World Radio POB 64 Manzini F. 1974

APPENDIX A

TANZANIA	*Daily News* POB 9033 Dar es Salaam F. 1972	*Radio Tanzania* POB 9191 Dar es Salaam F. 1956	Shihata POB 4755 Dar es Salaam
	Kipanga POB 199 Zanzibar	*Television Zanzibar* POB 314 Zanzibar	
	Uhuru POB 9221 Dar es Salaam	*The Voice of Tanzania Zanzibar* POB 1178 Zanzibar	
TOGO	*Journal Officiel de la Republique du Togo* BP 891, Lome	*Radiodiffusion Kara (Togo)* BP 21 Lama Kara	Agence Togolaise de Presse BP 2327 Lome F. 1975
	La Nouvelle Marche BP 891 Lome	*Radiodiffusion Television de la Nouvelle Marche* BP 434 Lome	
		Television Togolaise BP 3286, Lome F. 1973	
TUNISIA	*L'Action* 15 Rue 2 Mars 1934 Tunis F. 1932	*Radiodiffusion Television Tunisienne* 71 Ave de la Liberte Tunis	*Tunis Afrique Press (TAP)* 25 Ave du 7 Novembre Tunis

(TUNISIA)   *Al-Amal*
            15 Rue 2 Mars
            1934
            Tunis F. 1934

            Ach-Cha'ab
            29 Place Muhammed Ali
            Tunis F. 1985

            La Presse de Tunisie
            55 Ave. du 7 Novembre
            Tunis F. 1936

            As-Sabah
            4 Rue Ali Bach-Hamba
            Tunis

UGANDA   *Financial Times*   *Radio Uganda*   Uganda News
            POB 31399   POB 7142   Agency (UNA)
            Kampala   Kampala   POB 7142
                                                 Kampala
            Manno   *Uganda*
            POB 4027   *Television*
            Kampala   *Service*
                                POB 4260
            New Vision   Kampala
            POB 9815
            Kampala

            Ngabo
            POB 9362
            Kampala

APPENDIX A

(UGANDA)
: *Taifa Uganda Empya*
POB 1986
Kampala
F. 1953

The Star
POB 9362
Kampala
F. 1980

UPPER VOLTA
: *Notre Combat*
BP 584
Ouagadougou

ZAIRE
: *Boyoma*
31 Ave. Mobutu
Kisangani
Haute-Zaire

Elima
BP 11498 Kinshasa
F. 1928

Mjumbe
BP 2474
Lubumbashi
Shaba

Salongo
BP 601
Kinshasa / Limete

La Voix du Zaire
BP 3171 Kinshasa

Radio Candip
BP 373
Bunia

Zaire Television
BP 3171
Kinshasa-Gombe

Agence Zairose de Presse (AZAP)
BP 1595
Kinshasa I

Documentation et Informations Africaines
BP 1126
Kinshasa I

THE LEADING MEDIA INSTITUTIONS IN AFRICA

ZAMBIA	*The Times of Zambia* POB 30394 Lusaka F. 1943	*Zambia National Broadcasting Corp.* POB 50015 Lusaka F. 1966	Zambia News Agency (ZANA) Lusaka
	Zambia Daily Mail POB 31421 Lusaka F. 1968	Educational Broadcasting Services POB 50231 Lusaka	
ZIMBABWE	*The Chronicle* POB 585 Bulawayo F. 1894	*Zimbabwe Broadcasting* POB HG 444 Salisbury	Zimbabwe Inter-African News Agency (ZIANA) POB 8166 Park House, Salisbury
	The Herald POB 396 Salisbury	*Zimbabwe Television* POB HG 444 Salisbury	

157

appendix b

SELECTED RURAL NEWSPAPERS IN AFRICA

COUNTRY	NAME OF NEWSPAPER	LANGUAGE
Benin	Kparo	Bariba
	Eunbuke	Adja
	Imole	Yoruba
	Mi Se Nu	Fon
Burundi	Ubumwe	Kirundi
Cameroon	Bloc Note du Monde Rural	French
Central African Empire	Linga	Sengo
Congo	Sengo	French
	La Foret	French
Ghana	Kpodoga	Ewe
	Wonsuom	Fante
Côte d'Ivoire	Terre et Progres	French
	Agripomo	French
	La Nouvelle	French
Kenya	Kisomo	Kikuyu-Swahili
	Bumanyati	Swahili
Liberia	Gbehzohn Dukpa	English
	Maryland News	English

SELECTED RURAL NEWSPAPERS IN AFRICA

	Bong County News	
	Sonniequellie Sun	
	Lofa County Monthly	English
	Grand Gedeh News	
	Webbo World	English
	Ganta News	English
Mali	Kibaru	Bambara
Niger	Gangaa	Hausa
	Djerma	
	Saabon Ra'yii	Hausa
	Kasaa May Albarka	Hausa
	Amfaanin Kay	Hausa
	Alpishirinku	Hausa
	Is Ian Degn Tamajeq	Tamasheq
	Tarmaamum	Hausa
	Boro Coyo Gati Borcin	
	Tarey	Hausa/Zarma
	Jine Koy Yan	Zarma
	Mangaari Kuu Ye	Zarma
	Ililii Arzinin Kasaa	
	Albarkar Tsirkaw	
Rwanda	Hobe	Kinyarwanda
	Imvaho	Kinyarwanda
	Kinyamateka	Kinyarwanda
Zimbabwe	Mudzi District News	Shona

159

appendix c

AFRICA MEDIA FACTS BY REGION, 1990

African Telecommunications: West Region, p. 1
    Country: Sierra Leone
    Area: 71740 sq km
    Population: 3946000
    Population Density: 55.0 per sq km
    Radio Receivers: 830000
    TV Receivers: 33000
    Telephones: 13000
    Daily Newspapers: 1
    Average Circulation: 12000
    Radio Distribution: 4.75 persons per radio
    TV Distribution: 119.58 persons per tv
    Radio Date: 1934 or 1955
    TV Date: 1963
    Ownership: Government
    Programming/Uses: C; ED/NC; Home; BBC; VOA; Radio Moscow
    Media Type: Directed

African Telecommunications: West Region, p. 1
    Country: Togo
    Area: 56785 sq km

Population: 2747000
Population Density: 48.4 per sq km
Radio Receivers: 630000
TV Receivers: 12000
Telephones: 14000
Daily Newspapers: 2
Radio Distribution: 4.36 persons per radio
TV Distribution: 228.92 persons per tv
Radio Date: 1954
Ownership: Government
Programming/Uses: Homer services
Media Type: Unrestrained

African Telecommunications: West Region, p. 1
   Country: Nigeria
   Area: 923768 sq km
   Population: 104957000
   Population Density: 113.6 per sq km
   Radio Receivers: 7730000
   TV Receivers: 600000
   Telephones: 235000
   Daily Newspapers: 19
   Average Circulation:516000
   Radio Distribution: 13.58 person per radio
   TV Distribution: 194.92 persons per tv
   Radio Date: 1949
   TV Date: 1959
   Ownership: Public Corporations
   Programming/Uses: ED/NC; Sports; news; religion; music; commercial advertising
   Media Type: Unrestrained

African Telecommunications: West Region, p. 1
   Country: Senegal
   Area: 196722 sq km
   Population: 6881919
   Population Density: 35.0 per sq km
   Radio Receivers: 433000

APPENDIX C

TV Receivers: 7000
Telephones: 54000
Daily Newspapers: 3
Average Circulation: 53000
Radio Distribution: 15.89 persons per radio
TV Distribution: 983.13 persons per tv
Radio Date: 1939
TV Date: 1965
Ownership: Government
Programming/Uses: ED/NC; news; tv specifically for educational use
Media Type: Directed

African Telecommunications: West Region, p. 1
Country: Mauritania
Area: 1030700 sq km
Population: 1916000
Population Density: 1.9 per sq km
Radio Receivers: 206000
TV Receivers: 1000
Telephones: 12000
Radio Distribution: 9.30 persons per radio
TV Distribution: 1916 persons per tv
Radio Date: 1957
TV Date: 1984
Ownership: Government
Media Type: Restrained

African Telecommunications: West Region, p. 1
Country: Niger
Area: 1267000 sq km
Population: 7249596
Population Density: 5.7 per sq km
Radio Receivers: 324000
TV Receivers: 8000
Telephones: 12000
Daily Newspapers: 1
Average Circulation: 5000
Radio Distribution: 22.38 persons per radio

AFRICA MEDIA FACTS BY REIGION, 1990

TV Distribution: 906.2 persons per tv
Radio Date: 1958
TV Date: 1965
Ownership: Government
Programming/Uses: ED/NC; home plus network; imported programs
Media Type: Restrained

African Telecommunications: West Region, p. 1
  Country: Cape Verde
  Area: 4033 sq km
  Population: 334000
  Population Density: 83 per sq km
  Radio Receivers: 52000
  TV Receivers: 5000
  Telephones: 2000
  Radio Distribution: 6.42 persons per rdio
  TV Distribution: 66.8 persons per tv
  Ownership: Government
  Programming/Uses: Home services
  Media Type: Directed

African Telecommunications: West Region, p. 1
  Country: Gambia
  Area: 11295 sq km
  Population: 698817
  Population Density: 61.9 per sq km
  Radio Receivers: 110000
  Radio Distribution: 6.35 persons per radio
  Radio Date: 1962
  Ownership: Goverment/Private
  Programming/Uses: Home; BBC news
  Media Type: Directed

African Telecommunications: West Region, p. 1
  Country: Ghana
  Area: 238537 sq km
  Population: 13391000
  Population Density: 56.1 per sq km

APPENDIX C

Radio Receivers: 4000000
TV Receivers: 171000
Radio Distribution: 3.347 persons per radio
TV Distribution: 78.3 persons per tv
Radio Date: 1935
TV Date: 1965
Ownership: Government/Commercial
Programming/Uses: ED/NC; entertainment; music
Media Type: Directed

African Telecommunications: West Region, p. 1
Country: Guinea
Area: 245857 sq km
Population: 6225000
Population Density: 25 per sq km
Radio Receivers: 167000
TV Receivers: 11000
Daily Newspapers: 1
Average Circulation: 13000
Radio Distribution: 37.27 persons per radio
TV Distribution: 565.9 persons per tv
Radio Date: 1953
Ownership: Government
Programming/Uses: Home services
Media Type: Directed

African Telecommunications: West Region, p. 1
Country: Guinea-Bissau
Area: 36125 sq km
Population: 943000
Population Density: 26.1 per sq km
Radio Receivers: 38000
Daily Newspapers: 1
Average Circulation: 6000
Radio Distribution: 24.8 persons per radio
Ownership: Government
Programming/Uses: Home services
Media Type: Directed

AFRICA MEDIA FACTS BY REIGION, 1990

African Telecommunications: West Region, p. 1
    Country: Ivory Coast
    Area: 322462
    Population: 9742900
    Population Density: 30 per sq km
    Radio Receivers: 1300000
    TV Receivers: 500000
    Telephones: 88000
    Daily Newspapers: 1
    Average Circulation: 80000
    Radio Distribution: 7.49 persons per radio
    TV Distribution: 19.49 persons per tv
    Radio Date: 1949
    TV Date: 1963
    Ownership: Government
    Programming/Uses: ED/NC; News; development info; TV used heavily in ed project
    Media Type: Directed

African Telecommunications: West Region, p. 1
    Country: Liberia
    Area: 97754 sq km
    Population: 2349000
    Population Density: 24.0 per sq km
    Radio Receivers: 600000
    TV Receivers: 45000
    Daily Newspapers: 1
    Average Circulation: 8000
    Radio Distribution: 3.92 persons per radio
    TV Distribution: 52.2 persons per tv
    Radio Date: 1949
    TV Date: 1964
    Ownership: Government
    Programming/Uses: ED/NC; religious; cultural; news; music; political; VOA
    Media Type: Restrained

APPENDIX C

African Telecommunications: West Region, p. 1
   Country: Mali
   Area: 1240192 sq km
   Population: 7620225
   Population Density: 6.1 per sq km
   Radio Receivers: 300000
   TV Receivers: 1000
   Telephones: 13000
   Daily Newspapers: 2
   Average Circulation: 4000
   Radio Distribution: 25.40 persons per radio
   TV Distribution: 7620.22 persons per tv
   Radio Date: 1957
   Ownership: Government
   Programming/Uses: home services
   Media Type: Directed

African Telecommunications: West Region, p. 1
   Country: Benin
   Area: 112622 sq km
   Population: 4446000
   Population Density: 39.5 per sq km
   Radio Receivers: 310000
   TV Receivers: 16000
   Telephones: 16000
   Daily Newspapers: 1
   Average Circulation: 1000
   Radio Distribution: 14.34 persons per radio
   TV Distribution: 277.875 persons per tv
   Radio Date: 1961
   Ownership: Government
   Programming/Uses: home services
   Media Type: Restrained

African Telecommunications: West Region, p. 1
   Country: Burkina Faso
   Area: 274200 sq km
   Population: 8509000

AFRICA MEDIA FACTS BY REIGION, 1990

Population Density: 31.0 per sq km
Radio Receivers: 170000
TV Receivers: 38000
Telephones: 14000
Daily Newspapers: 1
Average Circulation: 2000
Radio Distribution: 50.05 persons per radio
TV Distribution: 223.92 persons per tv
Radio Date: 1959
TV Date: 1963
Ownership: Government
Programming/Uses: home; regional
Media Type: Directed

African Telecommunications: Central Region, p. 1
   Country: Sao Tome and Principe
   Area: 964 sq km
   Population: 108000
   Population Density: 112 per sq km
   Radio Receivers: 28000
   Radio Distribution: 3.86 persons per radio
   Radio Date: 1972
   Ownership: Government
   Media Type: Directed

African Telecommunications: Central Region, p. 1
   Country: Zaire
   Area: 2344885 sq km
   Population: 33458000
   Population Density: 14.3 per sq km
   Radio Receivers: 3400000
   TV Receivers: 20000
   Radio Distribution: 9.84 persons per radio
   TV Distribution: 1672.9 persons per tv
   Radio Date: 1936
   TV Date: 1966
   Ownership: Government
   Programming/Uses: C; ED/NC; religious; cultural; health; world affairs

APPENDIX C

   Media Type: Directed

African Telecommunications: Central Region, p. 1
   Country: Equatorial Guinea
   Area: 28051 sq km
   Population: 300000
   Population Density: 10.69 per sq km
   Radio Receivers: 103000
   TV Receivers: 2000
   Daily Newspapers: 1
   Average Circulation: 1000
   Radio Distribution: 2.91 persons per radio
   TV Distribution: 150 persons per tv
   TV Date: 1968
   Ownership: Government
   Programming/Uses: Home; cultural; commercial
   Media Type: Directed

African Telecommunications: Central Region, p. 1
   Country: Gabon
   Area: 267667 sq km
   Population: 1206000
   Population Density: 4.5 per sq km
   Radio Receivers: 125000
   TV Receivers: 24000
   Telephones: 14000
   Daily Newspapers: 0
   Average Circulation: 15000
   Radio Distribution: 9.64 persons per radio
   TV Distribution: 50.25 persons per tv
   Radio Date: 1959
   TV Date: 1963
   Ownership: Government
   Programming/Uses: ED/NC; TV trans. via satellite to other African
      countries
   Media Type: Directed

AFRICA MEDIA FACTS BY REIGION, 1990

African Telecommunications: Central Region, p. 1
   Country: Cameroon
   Area: 475442 sq km
   Population: 10821746
   Population Density: 22.8 per sq km
   Radio Receivers: 1250000
   Telephones: 47000
   Daily Newspapers: 1
   Average Circulation: 35000
   Radio Distribution: 8.65 persons per radio
   Radio Date: 1941
   TV Date: 1985
   Ownership: Government
   Programming/Uses: Home; international; porvincial; urban services
   Media Type: Unrestrained

African Telecommunications: Central Region, p. 1
   Country: Central African Republic
   Area: 622984
   Population: 2740000
   Population Density: 4.4 per sq km
   Radio Receivers: 158000
   TV Receivers: 5000
   Telephones: 16000
   Radio Distribution: 17.34 persons per radio
   TV Distribution: 548 persons per tv
   Radio Date: 1958
   TV Date: 1983
   Ownership: Government
   Media Type: Directed

African Telecommunications: Central Region, p. 1
   Country: Chad
   Area: 1259200 sq km
   Population: 5061000
   Population Density: 4 per sq km
   Radio Receivers: 1.2 million
   Radio Distribution: 4.21 persons per radio

169

APPENDIX C

   Radio Date: 1955
   Ownership: Government/Private
   Programming/Uses: Gov't Propaganda; clandestine radio
   Media Type: Directed

African Telecommunications: Central Region, p. 1
   Country: Congo
   Area: 342000 sq km
   Population: 1843421
   Population Density: 5.4 per sq km
   Radio Receivers: 116000
   TV Receivers: 6000
   Telephones: 23000
   Daily Newspapers: 1
   Average Circulation: 8000
   Radio Distribution: 15.89 persons per radio
   TV Distribution: 307.23 persons per tv
   Radio Date: 1935
   TV Date: 1963
   Ownership: Government
   Programming/Uses: TV 46 hrs/wk
   Media Type: Directed

African Telecommunications: East Region, p. 1
   Country: Tanzania
   Area: 945087 sq km
   Population: 22462000
   Population Density: 24 per sq km
   Radio Receivers: 549000
   TV Receivers: 15000
   Telephones: 111000
   Daily Newspapers: 2
   Average Circulation: 101000
   Radio Distribution: 40.91 persons per radio
   TV Distribution: 1497.47 persons per tv
   Radio Date: 1961
   Ownership: Government
   Programming/Uses: C; ED/ND

AFRICA MEDIA FACTS BY REIGION, 1990

Media Type: Unrestrained

African Telecommunications: East Region, p. 1
   Country: Uganda
   Area: 197058 sq km
   Population: 12630076
   Population Density: 52.4 per sq km
   Radio Receivers: 335000
   TV Receivers: 79000
   Telephones: 57000
   Daily Newspapers: 1
   Average Circulation: 25000
   Radio Distribution: 37.70 persons per radio
   TV Distribution: 159.87 persons per tv
   Radio Date: 1958
   TV Date: 1963
   Ownership: Government
   Programming/Uses: News; gov't propaganda
   Media Type: Restrained

African Telecommunications: East Region, p. 1
   Country: Somalia
   Area: 637657 sq km
   Population: 6860000
   Population Density: 10.8 per sq km
   Radio Receivers: 260000
   TV Receivers: 3000
   Radio Distribution: 26.38 persons per radio
   TV Distribution: 2286.66 persons per tv
   Radio Date: 1943
   Ownership: Government/Private
   Programming/Uses: ED/NC; C; clandestine radio
   Media Type: Restrained

African Telecommunications: East Region, p. 1
   Country: Sudan
   Area: 2505813 sq km
   Population: 20564364

APPENDIX C

  Population Density: 8.2 per sq km
  Radio Receivers: 5300000
  TV Receivers: 1200000
  Telephones: 68000
  Daily Newspapers: 6
  Average Circulation: 105000
  Radio Distribution: 3.9 persons per radio
  TV Distribution: 17.14 persons per tv
  Radio Date: 1940
  TV Date: 1962
  Ownership: Government
  Programming/Uses: C; ED/NC; News and politics; satellite station
  Media Type: Restrained

African Telecommunications: East Region, p. 1
  Country: Rwanda
  Area: 26338 sq km
  Population: 6274000
  Population Density: 219 per sq km
  Radio Receivers: 411735
  Telephones: 6235
  Radio Distribution: 15.24 persons per radio
  Radio Date: 1965
  Ownership: Government
  Programming/Uses: ED/NC
  Media Type: Restrained

African Telecommunications: East Region, p. 1
  Country: Seychelles
  Area: 454 sq km
  Population: 66229
  Population Density: 145.9 per sq km
  Radio Receivers: 30000
  TV Receivers: 7500
  Telephones: 5783
  Daily Newspapers: 1
  Average Circulation: 4000
  Radio Distribution: 2.20 persons per radio

AFRICA MEDIA FACTS BY REIGION, 1990

TV Distribution: 8.83 persons per tv
Radio Date: 1965
TV Date: 1983
Ownership: Government
Programming/Uses: ED/NC
Media Type: Directed

African Telecommunications: East Region, p. 1
   Country: Ethiopia
   Area: 1251282 sq km
   Population: 47882000
   Population Density: 38.3 per sq km
   Radio Receivers: 8.7 million
   TV Receivers: 70000
   Telephones: 116000
   Daily Newspapers: 3
   Average Circulation: 40000
   Radio Distribution: 5.50 persons per radio
   TV Distribution: 684.02 persons per tv
   Radio Date: 1941
   TV Date: 1964
   Ownership: Government
   Programming/Uses: Commerical; clandestine radio
   Media Type: Restrained

African Telecommunications: East Region, p. 1
   Country: Kenya
   Area: 580367 sq km
   Population: 21163000
   Population Density: 36.5 per sq km
   Radio Receivers: 1900000
   TV Receivers: 200000
   Radio Distribution: 11.14 persons per radio
   TV Distribution: 105.81 persons per tv
   Radio Date: 1928
   TV Date: 1962
   Ownership: Government
   Programming/Uses: C; News; current affaris; traditional music

APPENDIX C

　　Media Type: Directed

African Telecommunications: East Region, p. 1
　　Country: Burundi
　　Area: 27834 sq km
　　Population: 5149000
　　Population Density: 185.0 per sq km
　　Radio Receivers: 270000
　　TV Receivers: 1000
　　Telephones: 7000
　　Radio Distribution: 19.07 persons per radio
　　TV Distribution: 5147 persons per tv
　　Radio Date: 1960
　　Ownership: Government
　　Programming/Uses: News; entertainment
　　Media Type: Restrained

African Telecommunications: East Region, p. 1
　　Country: Djibouti
　　Area: 23200 sq km
　　Population: 483000
　　Population Density: 20.818 per sq km
　　Radio Receivers: 32000
　　TV Receivers: 14000
　　Telephones: 4452
　　Radio Distribution: 15.09 persons per radio
　　TV Distribution: 34.5 persons per tv
　　Radio Date: 1966
　　TV Date: 1967
　　Ownership: Government
　　Programming/Uses: ED/NC; news; Arab Satellite Communication Organi-
　　　　zation
　　Media Type: Directed

African Telecommunications: North Region, p. 1
　　Country: Libya
　　Area: 1775500 sq km
　　Population: 4232000

Population Density: 2 per sq km
Radio Receivers: 900000
TV Receivers: 255000
Radio Distribution: 4.70 persons per radio
TV Distribution: 16.6 persons per tv
Radio Date: 1957
TV Date: 1968
Ownership: Government
Programming/Uses: News; Propaganda; clandestine radio
Media Type: Restrained

African Telecommunications: North Region, p. 1
Country: Morocco
Area: 710850 sq km
Population: 23376000
Population Density: 32 per sq km
Radio Receivers: 5000000
TV Receivers: 1500000
Telephones: 325000
Daily Newspapers: 14
Radio Distribution: 4.7 persons per radio
TV Distribution: 15.6 persons per tv
Radio Date: before 1956
TV Date: 1954
Ownership: Government/Private
Programming/Uses: ED/NC; News; Voice of America
Media Type: Directed

African Telecommunications: North Region, p. 1
Country: Tunisia
Area: 154530 sq km
Population: 7809000
Population Density: 48 per sq km
Radio Receivers: 1693527
TV Receivers: 500000
Radio Distribution: 4.61 persons per radio
TV Distribution: 15.61 persons per tv
Radio Date: 1930

APPENDIX C

    TV Date: 1966
    Ownership: Government
    Programming/Uses: ED/NC; News; Gov't Prop.
    Media Type: Directed

African Telecommunications: Southern Region, p. 1
    Country: Angola
    Area: 1246700 sq km
    Population: 8989800
    Population Density: 7.4 per sq km
    Radio Receivers: 230000
    TV Receivers: 40000
    Telephones: 40000
    Daily Newspapers: 4
    Average Circulation: 112000
    Radio Distribution: 39.09 persons per radio
    TV Distribution: 224.74 persons per tv
    Ownership: Government
    Programming/Uses: C; ED/NC
    Media Type: Restrained

African Telecommunications: North Region, p. 1
    Country: Algeria
    Area: 2381741 sq km
    Population: 22971558
    Population Density: 9.6 per sq km
    Radio Receivers: 5000000
    TV Receivers: 1610000
    Telephones: 709000
    Daily Newspapers: 5
    Average Circulation: 570000
    Radio Distribution: 4.594 persons per radio
    TV Distribution: 14.268 persons per tv
    Radio Date: 1925
    TV Date: 1956
    Ownership: Government
    Programming/Uses: ED/NC; News
    Media Type: Directed

AFRICA MEDIA FACTS BY REIGION, 1990

African Telecommunications: North Region, p. 1
   Country: Egypt
   Area: 997728.5 sq km
   Population: 51897000
   Population Density: 52.0 per sq km
   Radio Receivers: 115.5 million
   TV Receivers: 4.15 million
   Radio Distribution: 3.348 persons per radio
   TV Distribution: 12.505 persons per tv
   Radio Date: 1926
   TV Date: 1960
   Ownership: Government
   Programming/Uses: ED/NC; Home service; commercial service
   Media Type: Directed

African Telecommunications: Southern Region, p. 1
   Country: Zambia
   Area: 752614 sq km
   Population: 7531119
   Population Density: 9 per sq km
   Radio Receivers: 550000
   TV Receivers: 110000
   Radio Distribution: 13.69 persons per radio
   TV Distribution: 68.46 persons per tv
   Radio Date: 1941
   TV Date: 1961
   Ownership: Government
   Programming/Uses: ED/NC; Talk shows; music; news; religion; children's programs
   Media Type: Directed

African Telecommunications: Southern Region, p. 1
   Country: Zimbabwe
   Area: 390759 sq km
   Population: 8880000
   Population Density: 22.7 per sq km
   Radio Receivers: 750000
   TV Receivers: 193000

APPENDIX C

   Telephones: 272000
   Daily Newspapers: 3
   Radio Distribution: 11.84 persons per radio
   TV Distribution: 46.01 persons per tv
   Ownership: Government
   Programming/Uses: light programs; educational programs; clandestine radio
   Media Type: Unrestrained

African Telecommunications: Southern Region, p. 1
   Country: South Africa
   Area: 1221037 sq km
   Population: 33849000
   Population Density: 28 per sq km
   Radio Receivers: 10600000
   TV Receivers: 3200000
   Telephones: 4236000
   Daily Newspapers: 20
   Average Circulation: 1128000
   Radio Distribution: 3.19 persons per radio
   TV Distribution: 10.58 persons per tv
   Radio Date: 1923
   TV Date: 1976
   Ownership: Government
   Programming/Uses: C; News; Entertainment; Sports; clandestine radio
   Media Type: Restrained

African Telecommunications: Southern Region, p. 1
   Country: Swaziland
   Area: 17363 sq km
   Population: 676089
   Population Density: 39 per sq km
   Radio Receivers: 105000
   TV Receivers: 9000
   Telephones: 16000
   Daily Newspapers: 2
   Average Circulation: 10000
   Radio Distribution: 6.44 persons per radio
   TV Distribution: 75.12 persons per tv

Radio Date: before 1968
Ownership: Government
Programming/Uses: C; ED/NC
Media Type: Directed

African Telecommunications: Southern Region, p. 1
Country: Reunion
Area: 2512 sq km
Population: 570000
Population Density: 227 per sq km
Radio Receivers: 120000
TV Receivers: 91200
Telephones: 107400
Daily Newspapers: 2
Average Circulation: 51000
Radio Distribution: 4.75 persons per radio
TV Distribution: 6.25 persons per tv
Ownership: Government/Private
Media Type: Directed

African Telecommunications: Southern Region, p. 1
Country: Saint Helena
Area: 122 sq km
Population: 5559
Population Density: 46 per sq km
Radio Receivers: 2000
Radio Distribution: 2.78 persons per radio
Ownership: Government
Programming/Uses: serves local residents only - 30 hrs/wk
Media Type: Directed

African Telecommunications: Southern Region, p. 1
Country: Malawi
Area: 118484 sq km
Population: 7982607
Population Density: 67.4 per sq km
Radio Receivers: 1500000
Radio Distribution: 5.32 persons per radio

APPENDIX C

    Radio Date: 1964
    Ownership: Government/Commercial
    Programming/Uses: C; ED/NC; agricultural ext. service; nationalism; news
    Media Type: Restrained

African Telecommunications: Southern Region, p. 1
    Country: Mauritius
    Area: 2040 sq km
    Population: 1036000
    Population Density: 504 per sq km
    Radio Receivers: 280000
    TV Receivers: 110000
    Telephones: 65000
    Daily Newspapers: 7
    Average Circulation: 50000
    Radio Distribution: 3.7 persons per radio
    TV Distribution: 9.4 persons per tv
    Radio Date: 1944
    TV Date: 1965
    Ownership: Government
    Programming/Uses: Commerical
    Media Type: Restrained

African Telecommunications: Southern Region, p. 1
    Country: Mozambique
    Area: 799380 sq km
    Population: 14174000
    Population Density: 18 per sq km
    Radio Receivers: 550000
    TV Receivers: 13000
    Telephones: 54000
    Daily Newspapers: 2
    Average Circulation: 81000
    Radio Distribution: 25.77 persons per radio
    TV Distribution: 1090.30 persons per tv
    Ownership: Government/Private
    Programming/Uses: C; ED/NC; music; drama; interviews; women's features
    Media Type: Restrained

AFRICA MEDIA FACTS BY REIGION, 1990

African Telecommunications: Southern Region, p. 1
    Country: Namibia
    Area: 824292 sq km
    Population: 1252000
    Population Density: 1.5 per sq km
    Radio Receivers: 210000
    TV Receivers: 18000
    Radio Distribution: 5.96 persons per radio
    TV Distribution: 69.5 persons per tv
    Ownership: Government
    Programming/Uses: ED/NC
    Media Type: Unrestrained

African Telecommunications: Southern Region, p. 1
    Country: Lesotho
    Area: 30355 sq km
    Population: 1619000
    Population Density: 53.3 per sq km
    Radio Receivers: 110000
    Radio Distribution: 14.7 persons per radio
    Radio Date: 1964
    Ownership: Government
    Programming/Uses: C; ED/NC
    Media Type: Directed

African Telecommunications: Southern Region, p. 1
    Country: Madagascar
    Area: 587041 sq km
    Population: 9985000
    Population Density: 17 per sq km
    Radio Receivers: 2108000
    TV Receivers: 100000
    Telephones: 37000
    Daily Newspapers: 5
    Average Circulation: 46000
    Radio Distribution: 4.74 persons per radio
    TV Distribution: 99.85 persons per tv
    Radio Date: 1931

APPENDIX C

TV Date: 1965
Ownership: Government
Programming/Uses: ED/NC
Media Type: Directed

African Telecommunications: Southern Region, p. 1
Country: Botswana
Area: 582000 sq km
Population: 1211816
Population Density: 2.1 per sq km
Radio Receivers: 150000
Telephones: 22000
Daily Newspapers: 1
Average Circulation: 18000
Radio Distribution: 8.08 persons per radio
Radio Date: 1972
Ownership: Government
Programming/Uses: ED/NC; BBC newsl farming info
Media Type: Unrestrained

African Telecommunications: Southern Region, p. 1
Country: Comoro Islands
Area: 1862 sq km
Population: 484000
Population Density: 260 per sq km
Radio Receivers: 54000
Radio Distribution: 8.96 persons per radio
Radio Date: 1975
Ownership: Government
Programming/Uses: home and international services
Media Type: Directed

appendix d

ELECTRONIC BROADCASTING BY REGION

West African Electronic Broadcasting

Country Population Area Density	Receivers in Use: Radio Television	Date System Began	Type of Ownership	Types of Programs/ Uses
Benin 4,042,000 112,622 sq km 36 per sq km	300,000 15,000	1961 —	Government	Home services

Future Plans: Interested in joining Intelsat.

| Burkina Faso
7,964,705
274,200 sq km
29 per sq km | 123,000
35,000 | 1959
1963 | Government | Home; Regional |

Future Plans: Public viewing centers are operational.

APPENDIX D

Cape Verde 334,000 4,033 sq km 83 per sq km	50,000 2,000	— —	Government	Home services

Future Plans: France has agreed to provide adi for radio and television.

Gambia 698,817 11,295 sq km 62 per sq km	105,000 —	1962 —	Government and private	Home; BBC news

Future Plans: Future plans focus on filmmaking and film exchange.

Ghana 14,045,000 238,537 sq km 59 per sq km	140,000 —	1935 1965	Government and private	ED/NC; Entertainment; Music

Guinea 6,225,000 245,857 sq km 25 per sq km	180,000 7,700	1953 —	Government	Home services

Guinea-Bissau 810,000 36,125 sq km 22 per sq km	25,000 —	— —	Government	Home services

Future Plans: Portugal funded an expermental TV service in 1988.

Ivory Coast 9,742,900 322,462 sq km 30 per sq km	1,300,000 500,000	1949 1963	Government	ED/NC; News; Development info; TV used heavily in education project

ELECTRONIC BROADCASTING BY REGION

Liberia 2,221,000 97,754 sq km 23 per sq km	500,000 43,000	1949 1964	Government	ED/NC; Religious; Cultural; News; Music; Political; Voice of America
Mali 7,620,225 1,240,000 sq km 6 per sq km	130,000 500	1957 —	Government	Home services
Mauritania 1,946,000 1,030,700 sq km 2 per sq km	250,000 500	1957 1984	Government	
Niger 5,686,000 1,267,000 sq km 4 per sq km	300,000 25,000	1958 1965	Government	ED/NC; Home plus network; imported programs

Future Plans: Radio/TV were to be restructured with World Bank assistance during the 1987-89 plan period. Plan to install 10,000 solar TV's at a rate of 450/year.

Nigeria 98,517,000 923,768 sq km 107 per sq km	8,100,000 500,000	1949 1959	Public corporation	ED/NC; Sports; News; Religion; Music; Commercial advertising

APPENDIX D

Senegal 6,397,000 196,192 sq km 33 per sq km	440,000 6,000	1939 1965	Government	ED/NC; News; TV specifically for educa- tional use
Sierra Leone 3,517,530 71,740 sq km 49 per sq km	700,000 25,000	1955 1963	Government	Commercial; ED/NC; Home; BBC; Voice of America; Radio Mos- cow
Togo 2,747,000 56,785 sq km 48 per sq km	610,000 15,000	1954 —	Government	Home ser- vices

Future Plans: Interested in joining Intelsat.

CENTRAl AfRicAN ElECTRONic bROAdCASTINq

Country Population Area Density	Receivers in Use: Radio Television	Date System Began	Type of Ownership	Types of Programs/ Uses
Cameroon 10,446,000 475,442 sq km 22 per sq km	940,000 —	1941 1985	Government	Home; Urban; International; Provincial

Future Plans: In 1988, 22 of 32 proposed television transmitters were in use with the remaining expected to become fully operational by the end of the same year.

Central African Republic 2,740,000 622,984 sq km 4 per sq km	150,000 1,400	1958 1983	Government	
Chad 5,061,000 1,259,200 sq km 4 per sq km	1,050,000 —	1955 —	Government & Private	Government propaganda; Clandestine radio

Future Plans: USSR had agreed to establish TV services by the end of 1972.

Congo 1,912,429 342,000 sq km 6 per sq km	100,000 4,500	1935 1963	Government	

Future Plans: In 1988, signed an agreement to train Congolese personnel in USSR.

APPENDIX D

Equatorial Guinea 300,000 28,051 sq km 11 per sq km	100,000 2,200	— 1968	Government	Commercial; Home; Cultural
Gabon 1,206,000 267,667 sq km 11 per sq km	102,000 20,000	1959 1963	Government	ED/NC; TV trans. via satellite to other African countries.

Future Plans: Proposed 13 new FM radio stations and 13 new TV stations in 1986.

Sao Tome and Principe 108,000 964 sq km 112 per sq km	28,000 —	1972 —	Government	
Zaire 32,460,000 2,344,885 sq km 14 per sq km	525,000 15,000	1936 1966	Government	Commercial; ED/NC; religious; cultural; health; world affairs

EAST AFRICAN ELECTRONIC BROADCASTING

Country Population Area Density	Receivers in Use: Radio Television	Date System Began	Type of Ownership	Types of Programs/ Uses
Burundi 4,852,000 27,834 sq km 174 per sq km	180,000 250	1960 —	Government	Entertainment; News
Future Plans: Interested in joining Intelsat.				
Djibouti 456,000 23,200 sq km 20 per sq km	23,000 11,000	1966 1967	Government	ED/NC; News; Arab Satellite Communication Organization
Ethiopia 46,180,000 1,251,282 sq km 37 per sq km	3,000,000 50,000	1941 1964	Government	Commercial; Clandestine radio
Kenya 21,163,000 580,367 sq km 36 per sq km	3,400,000 250,000	1928 1962	Government	Commercial; News; Current affairs; Traditional music
Rwanda 5,757,000 26,338 sq km 00 per sq km	250,000 —	1965 —	Government	ED/NC
Future Plans: Interested in joining Intelsat.				

APPENDIX D

Seychelles 66,229 454 sq km 146 per sq km	16,000 5,000	1965 1983	Government	ED/NC
Somalia 4,760,000 637,657 sq km 7 per sq km	134,000 1,000	1943 —	Government & Private	Commercial; ED/NC; Clandestine radio
Sudan 20,564,364 2,505,813 sq km 00 per sq km	5,400,000 1,100,000	1940 1962	Government	Commercial; ED/NC; News and politics; Satellite station
Tanzania 22,462,000 945,087 sq km 24 per sq km	591,000 11,000	1961 —	Government	Commerical; ED/NC
Uganda 12,630,076 197,058 sq km 64 per sq km	320,000 81,000	1958 1963	Government	News; Government propaganda

ELECTRONIC BROADCASTING BY REGION

North African Electronic Broadcasting

Country Population Area Density	Receivers in Use: Radio Television	Date System Began	Type of Ownership	Types of Programs/ Uses
Algeria 22,971,558 2,381,741 sq km 10 per sq km	4,800,000 1,557,000	1925 1956	Government	ED/NC; News
Egypt 49,609,000 997,729 sq km 50 per sq km	12,000,000 3,860,000	1926 1960	Government	ED/NC; Commercial; Home service
Libya 3,624,000 1,775,500 sq km 2 per sq km	800,000 235,000	1957 1968	Government	News; Propaganda; Clandestine radio
Morocco 22,476,000 710,850 sq km 32 per sq km	3,850,000 1,206,000	1928 1954	Government radio & TV; Gov't TV	Commercial; ED/NC; News; Voice of America

Future Plans: A private television company intended to begin transmission in 1989.

| Tunisia
7,464,900
154,530 sq km
48 per sq km | 1,150,000
400,000 | 1930
1966 | Government | ED/NC;
News; Gov't propaganda |

191

APPENDIX D

SOUTHERN AFRICAN ELECTRONIC BROADCASTING

Country Population Area Density	Receivers in Use: Radio Television	Date System Began	Type of Ownership	Types of Programs/ Uses
Angola 8,989,800 1,246,700 sq km 7 per sq km	230,000 33,000	— —	Government	Commercial; ED/NC
Botswana 1,131,000 582,000 sq km 2 per sq km	140,000 —	1972 —	Government	ED/NC; BBC news; Farming info

Future Plans: Commercial radio network under consideration; National TV service under consideration.

Comoro Islands 484,000 1,862 sq km 260 per sq km	54,000 —	1975 —	Government	Home and international services

Future Plans: In 1986, France announced that it would fund the construction of a TV station.

Lesotho 1,528,000 30,000 sq km 50 per sq km	300,000 —	1964 —	Government	C; ED/NC
Madagascar 9,985,000 587,041 sq km 17 per sq km	2,000,000 96,000	1931 1965	Government	ED/NC

ELECTRONIC BROADCASTING BY REGION

Malawi 7,278,925 118,484 sq km 61 per sq km	1,060,000 —	1964 —	Government and Com- mercial	Commercial; ED/NC; Agricultural extension service
Mauritius 1,029,000 2,040 sq km 504 per sq km	250,000 128,111	1944 1965	Government	Commercial
Mozambique 14,174,000 799,380 sq km 18 per sq km	450,000 6,500	— —	Government & Private	Commercial; ED/NC; Music; Drama; Inter- views; Women's fea- tures
Namibia 1,184,000 824,269 sq km 1 per sq km	52,255 24,555	— —	Government	serves local residents
Reunion 570,000 2,512 sq km 227 per sq km	120,000 91,200	— —	Government & Private	
Saint Helena 5,559 122 sq km 46 per sq km	2,000 —	— —	Government	serves local residents only

APPENDIX D

South Africa 33,849,000 1,221,037 sq km 28 per sq km	10,000,000 3,000,000	1923 1976	Government	Commercial; News; Entertainment; Sports; Clandestine radio
Swaziland 676,089 17,363 sq km 38.9 per sq km	96,000 12,400	1968 —	Government	Commercial; ED/NC
Zambia 6,730,000 752,614 sq km 9 per sq km	1,000,000 240,000	1941 1961	Government	ED/NC; Talk shows; music; news; religion; children's programs
Zimbabwe 8,640,000 390,759 sq km 22 per sq km	375,000 112,000	— —	Government	Light programs; Educational programs; Clandestine radio

REFERENCES

Abadoe, Mathis. "Immediate Freedom of the Press in the Emergent Nations: Yes or No?" *The Journalists World*, Vol. 3, No. 1, 1965.

Abaoba, D. *The Nigerian Press Under Military Rule*. Buffalo: State University of New York, unpublished doctoral dissertation, 1979.

Ainslie, Rosalynde. *The Press in Africa: Communications Past and Present*. London: Gollancz, 1966.

Aithnard, K. M. *The Cultural Policy of Togo*. Paris: UNESCO, 1976.

Ansah, P., Fall, C., Kouley, B., Mwaura, P. *Rural Journalism in Africa*. Paris: UNESCO, 1981.

Appiah, M. A. *Okyeame: An Integrative Model of Communication Behavior*. Buffalo: State University of New York, unpublished doctoral dissertation, 1979.

Asante, M. and Appiah, M., "The Rhetoric of the Akan Drum," *Western Journal of Black Studies*, Fall, 1978.

Asante, M., Noack, G., Nyahunvi, and Lewin, H., *Media Training Needs in Zimbabwe*. Harare: Mass Media Trust, 1982 (Unpublished Report).

Ayers, R. U. *Technological Forecasting and Long Range Planning*. New York: McGraw-Hill, 1969.

Barton, Frank, *The Press in Africa*. London: MacMillan, 1979.

Bennett, Norman. *Africa and Europe*. New York: Africana Publishing, 1975.

Black, Jay and Whitney, Fredrick C. *Introduction to Mass Communication*. Dubuque, Iowa: William C. Brown, 1983, 1988.

Budge, E. A. W. *Egyptian Language*. New York: Dover, 1983.

REFERENCES

"Building A Pan African Communications Network," *Africa Report*, Vol. 17, April, 1972.
Cassata, M. and Asante, M. *Mass Communication: Principles and Practices*. New York: MacMillan, 1979.
Chimutengwende, Chenhamo. *South Africa: The Press and the Politics of Liberation*. London: Barbican, 1978.
Chimutengwende, Chenhamo, "The Role of the Mass Media in African Development," *African Finance*, April 1, 1981.
Coker, O. S., "Mass Media in Nigeria," in ed. Royal D. Colle. *Mass Media Systems*. Ithaca, New York: Cornell University Press, 1968.
Coleman, James. "The Politics of Sub-Saharan Africa," in ed. Gabriel Almond and James Coleman, *The Politics of the Developing Areas*. Princeton, N.J.: Princeton University Press, 1960.
Diop, C. A. *Civilisation ou Barbarie*. Paris: Presence Africaine, 1983.
Dodson, O. and Hachten, W. "Communication and Development: African and Afro-American Parallels," *Journalism Monographs*, No. 29, May 1973.
Elias, T. O. *Nigerian Press Law*. Oxford: Oxford University Press, 1969.
Ezera, Kalu. *Constitutional Development in Nigera*. Cambridge: Cambridge University Press, 1964.
Foster, Philip, "Problems of Educational Development," in *Africa: South of the Sahara: 1980–81*. London: Europa, 1980.
Goldberg, Mel. Personal interview, New York, June 12, 1984.
Hachten, William, "Newspapers in Africa: Change or Decay," *Africa Report*, December, 1970.
Herald, May 29, 1982.
Holland, J., "Freedom of the Press in the Commonwealth," in ed. G. O. Onogoruwa, *Press Freedom in Crisis: A Study of the Amakiri Case*. Ibadon: Sketch Publishing, 1978.
Howarth, T., "Taking a Stand for Computers in Education," *Personal Computing*, May, 1983.
Innis, H. *Empire and Communications*. Toronto: 1972.
James, George, *Stolen Legacy*. San Francisco, Richardson Associates, 1978.
Jahn, Janheinz, *Muntu: The New African Culture*. New York: Grove, 1961.
Kangai, Tarivafi. Personal interview, Harare, Zimbabwe, February, 1982.
Katz, Elihu and George Wedell. *Broadcasting in the Third World*. Cambridge: Harvard University Press, 1977.

REFERENCES

Legum, Colin, "The Mass Media Institutions of the African Political Systems," in ed. Olav Stokke, *Reporting Africa*. Uppsala: Scandinavian Institute of African Studies, 1971.

Legum, Colin, ed. *Africa Contemporary Record: Annual Survey and Documents*. New York: Africana Publishing, 1973.

Lindenau, S. E. "Lights and Wires in a Box: The Computer-Oriented Information Age in Support of Effective Higher Education." *Educational Technology*, February, 1984.

Lerner, Daniel. *The Passing of Traditional Society: Modernizing in the Middle East*. New York: The Free Press, 1958.

Lugard, Frederick, *The Dual Mandate*. London, 1922.

Mahbul, Hag. *The Poverty Curtain*. New York: Columbia University Press, 1976.

Makunike, Ezekiel. *The Sharpener*, Vol. 1, No. 1, July/Aguust, 1981.

Mannheim, Karl. *Ideology and Utopia*. London, 1972.

Malinowski, B., "The Dynamics of Social Change." In ed., E. Wallerstein, *Social Change: The Colonial Situation*. New York: Wiley and Sons, 1966.

Mass Media in an African Context. Paris: UNESCO, 1974.

Mbanga, Wilf. Personal interview, Harare, Zimbabwe, February 10, 1982.

Marere, M. A. Personal interview, Harare, Zimbabwe, February 10, 1982.

Metrowich, F. R., "The Press in Africa: Muffled Drums," *Africa Institute Bulletin*, Vol. 13, nos. 9 & 10, 1975.

Munyuki, Farayi. Personal interview, Harare, Zimbabwe, December 19, 1981.

Musarurwa, Willie, "Press Responsibility in a Developing Country," in ed. Molefi Asante, *International Press Seminar*. Harare, Zimbabwe: Ranche House, 1981.

Nhiwatiwa, N. P. *International Communication Between the European and African World Views*. Buffalo: State University of New York, unpublished doctoral dissertation, 1979.

Nehru, Jawaharal. "The Discovery of India," in ed. Emmanuel Wallerstein, *The Social Change: The Colonial Situation*. New York: Wiley and Sons, 1966.

Obotette, Bassey. *The Nigerian Press and Political Integration*. Washington: Howard University, unpublished doctoral dissertation, 1984.

Omu, Fred, "The Dilemma of Press Freedom in Colonial Africa: The West Africa Example," *Journal of African History*, Vol. 9, No. 2, 1968.

Omu, Fred. *Press and Politics in Nigeria 1880–1937*. Atlantic Highlands, N.J.: Humanities Press, 1978.

REFERENCES

Opubor, Alfred. Personal interview, Bellagio, Italy, Aguust 1979.
Opubor, Alfred. Personal interview, Dakar, Senegal, December 20, 1981.
Pelton, J. W. "The Future of Telecommunications: A Delphi Study."*Journal of Communications*, Winter, 1981.
Polcyn, K. A. "The Use of Communications Satellites for the Delivery of Education and Training Service: A Brief History and a Look at the Present and Future." *Journal of Educational Systems*, Vol. 8, No. 2, 1979–80.
Pollack, Richard. *Up Against Apartheid: The Role and Plight of the Press in South Africa*. Carbondale, Illinois: Southern Illinois University Press, 1980.
Pye, Lucien W., "Communication, Institution Building and the Reach of Authority," in D. Lerner and W. Schramm, eds. *Communications and Change in the Developing Countries*. Honolulu: East-West Center Press, 1971.
Pye, Lucien. *Communications and Political Development*. Princeton, N.J.: Princeton University Press, 1963.
Rattray, R. *Ashanti*. Oxford: Oxford University Press, 1923.
Rodney, W. *How Europe Underdeveloped Africa*. Washington, D.C.: Howard University Press, 1974.
Rogers, Everett (ed.) *Communication and Development*. Beverly Hills: Sage, 1976.
Rubin, Barry. *International News and The American Media*. Beverly Hills: Sage, 1977.
Schiller, Herbert. *Communication and Cultural Domination*. White Plains: Sharpe, 1976.
Schramm, Wilbur, "The Soviet Communist Theory of the Press," in eds. F. S. Siebert, T. Peterson and W. Schramm, *Four Theories of the Press*. Urbana: University of Illinois Press, 1956.
Schramm, Wilbur. *Mass Media and National Development*. Stanford: Stanford University Press, 1964.
Sitaram, K. S. "Communications Satellites and Intercultural Understanding." Paper prepared at the Center for Advancing of Intercultural Communications, University of Guam, 1982.
Sitaram, K. S. "Communications Technology and Educational Development in Asia and the Pacific: Case Studies from India, Japan and Guam." Paper presented a a conference on Communications, Mass Media and Development, Northwestern University, Chicago, Illinois, November, 1983.
Sommerlad, E. L. *The Press in Developing Countries*. Sydney: Sydney University Press, 1966.
Spicer, J. "Media in Sudan," in M. Asante, ed. *Press Seminar Proceedings*. Harare: Ranche House, 1982.

REFERENCES

Stonier, T. "Making the Most of a Switched-On Society." *Times Higher Education Supplement*, Vol. 13, May, 1983.

The Europa World Year Book 1990 (Vols. I and II), Europa Publications Limited, 18 Bedford Square, London. WC1B 3JN, England.

The Role of Communication Media and Information Services in Population Related Development Programmes in Africa: A Report of Export Meeting. Nairobi: UNESCO Regional Population Unit for Africa, 1979.

The Role of Communication Media and Information Services. Paris: UNESCO, 1979.

Thiam, Cire, "A Decade After Independence: Two Africas Meet," International Press Institute Report, April, 1971.

Thomsen, D. E. "Light Conversations New York to D.C." *Science News*, Vol. 123, No. 5, January, 1983.

Vambe, Lawrence. Personal interview, Harare, Zimbabwe, December 19, 1981.

Wauthier, Claude, The Literature and Thought of Modern Africa. London: Heinemann, 1964.

Windrich, Elaine. *The Mass Media in the Struggle for Zimbabwe.* Gweru: Mambo Press, 1981.

Wilcox, Dennis L. *Mass Media in Black Africa.* New York: Praeger Publishing, 1975.

Wilson, J. A. *The Culture of Ancient Egypt.* Chicago: University of Chicago Press, 1978.

Ziegler, Dhyana, "The Use of Telecommunications Technology in Education: Opinions of Public Broadcasters, Educators and The National Aeronautics and Space Administration." *Doctoral Dissertation*, Southern Illinois University-Carbondale, 1985.

index

Abaabo, D., 39, 78–80, 102, 104–107
Abadoe, Mathis, 37
Access Restraints, 87–88
Addis Ababa Conference (1961), 44
African Drum, 6, 52
African Newspapers: Early, 11–15, Rural, 44–45, 47, 49
African Newsprint, 95
African Printing, 7–8, 11
African Regions: Central, 64, 167–170, 187–188, Eastern, 64, 170–174, 188–189, Northern, 65, 174–177, 191, Southern, 65–66, 177–182, 192–194, Western, 63–64, 160–167, 183–186
African Script, 7–8
Afrocentric Perspective, 4
Agence-France Presse, 114, 122
Ainslie, Rosalynde, 14, 17, 61–62
Aithnard, K.M., 4
Akan, 7
Algeria, 131–132
Algerie Presse Service (APS), 120

Angola, 35, 48, 132
Ansah, P., 45, 47–48, 100, 115
Appiah, M.A., 6, 7
Asante, M.K., 6, 110, 128
Associated Press, 114, 122
Ayers, R.U., 69

BAMUN Script, 8
Bantu Administration Act, 81
Barton, Frank, 11, 97, 102, 120
Belgian Colonies, 16, 21–23
Benin (Dahomey), 14, 35, 132, 158
Bennett, Norman, 15, 21–25
Black, Jay, 103
Botswana, 37, 132
British Broadcasting Corporation (BBC), 97
British Central Office of Information, 97
British Colonies, 13, 16, 19–20
Budge, E.A.W., 6
Burkina, 133
Burundi, 133, 158

201

INDEX

Cable News Network (CNN), 124
Cameroon, 133, 158
Canadian Broadcasting Corp., 97
Cape Verde, 133–134
Cassata, M., 128
Central African Republic, 49, 134
Central News Agency (CNA), 87
Chad, 30–31, 37, 134
Characteristics of African Media, 97–101
Chief Abiola, 29
Chimutengwende, Chenhamo, 41, 43, 81–82, 84, 87
Coker, O. S., 120
Coleman, James, 25
Colonial Press, 23–26
Colonialism, 3, 15
Comoros, 134
Congo (Belgium Congo) 35, 48, 134–135
Cote D'Ivoire, 40, 158
Criminal Law Amendment Act, 83
   Criminal Procedure and Evidence Act, 83
Culture, 4–5, 7
Customs and Excise Act, 86

Defense Amendment Act, 86
Didactic Media, 54
Diop, C.A., 5
Djibouti, 135
Dodson, O., 5

Egypt, 5–6, 9, 11, 92–93, 135–136
Electronic Media: Charteristics, 59–61, Control, 61–63
Elias, T.O., 108
Equatorial Guinea, 136

Ethiopia, 14, 136–137
European Influence, 4, 26, 40
European Printing Press, 11
Extension of University Education Act, 85
Ezera, Kalu, 77

Faso, 133
Folk Media, 53–54
Foster, Phillip, 44
Freedom & Responsibility, 128–130
Freedom Journal, 12
French Colonies, 13, 15–19
Frey, Frederick, 38

Gabon, 137
Gambia, 35, 137
German Colonies, 16, 23
Ghana (Gold Coast), 12–13, 35, 47, 92, 137, 158
Goldberg, Mel, 73
Guinea, 138
Guinea-Bissau, 138

Hachten, William, 5, 10, 27, 91
Hieroglyphics, 6, 9
Holland, J., 107
Howarth, T., 73
Hsinhua, 122

Innis, H., 9
International Telecommunications Satellite Organization (INTELSAT) 65, 72
Italian Colonies, 16, 23
Ivory Coast, 138

Jahn, Janheinz, 52

INDEX

The Jamahirijah Arab Revolutionary News Agency (ARNA), 120
James, George, 6
Japan Influence, 4

Kangai, Tirivafi, 57
Katz, Elihu, 41
Kenya, 40, 50, 93–94, 138–139, 158
Kenyan Institute for Mass Communication, 101
Kenyan Micro Publishing Unit (micro-pu), 48
King, Njoya, 8

Legum, Colin, 61, 91
Lerner, Daniel, 44
Lesotho, 139
Liberia, 14, 45, 139–140, 158
Libya, 140
Lindenau, S.E., 67
Lugard, Frederick, 19

Mada-Gascar, 140–141
Mahbul, Hag, 44
Makunike, Ezekiel, 37, 50, 100
Malawi, 141
Mali, 13, 45, 159
Mali National Agency of Information (ANIM), 45
Malinowski, B., 3
Mannheim, Karl, 126
Marere, M.A., 125
Mauritania, 141
Mauritius, 142–143
Mbanga, Wilf, 120
Media Control/Government Control, 29–31, 40

Media Problems, 92–95
Media Training Institutions, 51
Metrowick, F.R., 96, 102
Ministries for Literacy, 49
Morocco, 143–144
Mozambique, 35, 46, 48, 54, 144
Multi-Linguality, 56, 96
Munyuki, Farayi, 42
Musarurwa, Willie, 34–36, 115

Namibia, 35, 145
Nathan Shamuyarira, 4, 28, 33
National Development, 34, 36–44
National News Agencies, 119–120
Nehru, Jawaharal
New Alphabeth, 8
News Agencies, 114–118
The News Agency of Nigeria (NAN), 120–121
Newspaper and Imprint Registration Act, 87
Nhiwatiwa, N.P., 7
Niger, 13, 45, 145, 159
Nigeria, 13, 35, 37, 39, 50, 75–80, 107–109, 145–149
Nigerian Newspaper, 79
Nonimo, 9
Nordenstreng, Kaaele, 41

Obotette, Bassey, 37, 75–80
Official Secrets Act, 84, 108
Okyeame, 7
Omu, Fred, 26, 75, 78
Opubor, Alfred, 100, 115
Organization of African Units (OAU), 122–123
Oziri, H.M.

203

INDEX

Pan African News Agency (PANA), 120–125
Papyrus, 5
Pelton, J.W., 69
Polcyn, K.A., 72
Pollak, Richard, 90
Portuguese Colonies, 16, 21–23
Post Office Act, 84
Pre-Colonial, 8–10
Press Control, 106
Press Freedom, 39, 106
Press Theory, 103–104
Prison Act, 84
Production Costs, 96
Public Safety Act, 82–83
Publications and Entertainment Act, 85
Pye, Lucien, 38, 104

Radio, 53, 55–58, 97
Radio Moscow, 97
Radio Peking, 97
Ranganath, H.K.
Rattray, R., 6
Reunion, 149
Reuters, 114
Rhodesia Herald, 31–34, 42
Riotous Assemblies Act, 84
Rodney, W., 3
Rogers, Everett, 38, 41, 43–44
Rubin, Barry, 122
Rwanda, 48, 149, 159

Sahraro, 44
Sao Tome, 150
Satellites, 66–67
Schiller, Herbert, 114

Schramm, Wilbur, 38, 41, 44, 64, 103
Sean McBride Commission, 125
Seditious Offenses Bill, 26
Senegal, 45
Sertima, I.V.
Seychelles, 150
Shamuyarira, Nathan, 4, 28, 33
Sierra Leone, 11, 150
Sitaram, K.S., 72
Somalia, 150–151
Sommerland, E.L., 104
South Africa, 80–81, 95, 151–152
South African Press Association (SAPA), 33, 87, 110, 119
Spanish Colonies, 16, 23
Spicer, J., 130
The Steyn Commission, 89–90
Stonier, T., 73–74
Sudan, 13, 152–153
Suggestion of Communism Act, 82
Swaziland, 153

Tanzania, 35, 47–49, 154
Tass, 122–123
Technique, 69–70
Technological Forecasting: Delphi Technique, 69, Pyramid Technique, 69–70
Technological Problems, 67–69
Telecommunications Technologies, 70–74
Television, 53, 56, 97
Television, 58–59, 150
Thiam, Cire, 43
Thomsen, D.E., 73
Togo, 4, 45, 49, 154

INDEX

Transnational News Agencies, 114–118
The Tunis Afrique Press (TAP), 120
Tunisia, 154–155

Uganda, 155–156
UNESCO, 48, 52, 101, 121–122
Unilateral Declaration of Indepence (UDI), 27
United Nations Development Programme (UNDP), 48
United Press International, 114, 122
Upper Volta, 156

Vambe, Lawrence, 25, 28
Voice of American (VOA), 97

Wauthier, Claude, 13
Wedell, George, 4

Whitney, Frederick C., 103
Wilcox, Dennis, 3, 20, 25–26, 39, 61–62, 98, 114, 117, 124
Wilson, J.A., 5
Windrick, Elaine, 27

Zaire, 35, 156
Zambia, 48, 50, 94, 157
Ziegler, Dhyana, 70
Zimbabwe, 4, 7, 31, 33, 35, 37, 47–48, 50, 54 (Rhodesia), 109–113, 157, 159
Zimbabwe Broadcasting Corp. (ZBC), 57, 112–113, 119, 127
Zimbabwe Institute of Mass Communication, 37, 41, 46, 110, 113
Zimbabwe Inter African News Agency (ZIANA), 42, 110–111, 119–120
Zimbabwe Mass Media Trust, 110

P
92
.A35
Z54
1992

Ziegler, Dhyana.
Thunder and silence

		DATE DUE		